# RHYMNEY MEMORIES

BY
THOMAS JONES, C.H.

ABERYSTWYTH
THE NATIONAL LIBRARY OF WALES
1990

*Everyone has a lurking wish to appear considerable in his native place.*

*No place cured a man's vanity or arrogance so well as London.* Dr. Johnson.

A facsimile reprint of the first edition published by The Welsh Outlook Press, Newtown, 1938.

Cover illustration: portrait of Thomas Jones by William Rothenstein, 1923.

ISBN: 0-907158-43-9

TO MY SISTERS
ELIZABETH JONES
AND
HARRIET McKENZIE

# FOREWORD

D r. Thomas Jones C.H., LL.D., was born at 100, High Street, Rhymney, on 27th September, 1870. When his father later became a manager of the Company shop, the family moved to a row of more spacious houses provided for senior staff. The Terrace still stands solidly on the flat land, down the hill, almost opposite the railway station. Close by stands a club house owned by Messrs. Whitbread, which was once part of the Rhymney 'superstore' of the Victorian and Edwardian era. A visit to this building, then used as a centre for the unemployed, was the last public engagement outside London undertaken by Edward VIII prior to his abdication in 1936.

Tom was the eldest of nine children; he was known as Tom Jones Five at school, and later as T.J. to most of his friends. The family was well respected in town and chapel, but in 1870 who would have thought that after leaving Lewis School, Pengam, aged thirteen, and working as a wages clerk in the Company office until he was twenty years of age, Tom Jones would proceed via the Universities of Wales, Glasgow and Belfast, to Whitehall, to serve from 1916 to 1930 under four prime ministers as Deputy Secretary to the Cabinet? That story has been told in three volumes of his *Whitehall Diaries* published in 1968 by Oxford University Press. His *Diary with Letters* describes his later career when he became secretary of the Pilgrim Trust and the President of the University College at Aberystwyth. He was founder of Coleg Harlech, chairman of the Gregynog Press and author of a number of books on Welsh topics. He died aged 85 years in 1955.

It all began in Rhymney. As Librarian of the National Library of Wales, I am proud that we hold the Thomas Jones archive, made over to us in 1986 by T.J.'s surviving children, Baroness White of Rhymney, formerly M.P. for East Flint, and Tristan Jones, formerly manager of 'The Observer' newspaper.

We have been pleased to produce this special edition of T.J.'s *Rhymney Memories*, written in 1938, to mark the coming of the National Eisteddfod of Wales to the place of his birth.


Aberystwyth 1990

Brynley F. Roberts
Librarian
National Library of Wales

# PREFACE

IN 1932 I was asked to contribute to a series of articles which appeared in the *Times* reviewing the life of the previous fifty years. Recently I was asked to broadcast a similar review of life in Wales. A holiday last August as the guest of my friend Dr. Abraham Flexner in his peaceful Canadian camp on Lake Ahmic, Magnetawan, provided the leisure to expand these summaries into the sketch which follows. " This was my world ", a generation earlier than Lady Rhondda's, and " the other half " of hers. I have confined myself to one small village and to the years of my own childhood and youth before the dawn of the twentieth century, before the Great War; an age which knew nothing of the motor car, the gramophone, the wireless, the cinema, the telephone, the typewriter or the aeroplane, nothing of lipstick, cigarettes and cocktails. And I have written primarily for old friends and contemporaries in the Rhymney Valley, some of whom have acted as prompters, and for their children ; a fact or paragraph here and there may be of interest to other South Walians and to some future historian of the life of the common people in the nineteenth century.

In my boyhood I went to a church bazaar and plunged a hand deep into a cask full of sawdust and drew a prize at a venture. The cask was labelled Lucky Dip. In the pages which follow I play the game once more.

T. J.

STREET ACRE,
    ST. NICHOLAS-AT-WADE,
        THANET.

June, 1938.

# THANKS

A History of Rhymney and Pontlottyn, by J. S. Jones, was published in 1904 in Welsh and I have drawn on it for Chapter I. For the same chapter I have read, besides old newspaper files, three unpublished theses by university graduates :—

The Economic Industrial and Social History of Ebbw Vale 1775-1927, by Arthur Gray Jones.

Movements towards Social Reform in South Wales, 1832-1850, by Lillian Williams.

History of Transport in Monmouth, by Mary Alma Swallow.

The result is a chapter which is neither fish, flesh, nor fowl, but kedgeree. Perhaps some Rhymney graduate with more leisure than I have for research will work over this ground thoroughly.

Among friends to whom I am indebted for varied assistance I must mention Timothy Davies, Tom Evans, Gomer Jones, W. J. Jones, D. G. Lloyd and W. H. Trump, all of Rhymney; James Davies, Caerphilly ; David Williams and D. E. Evans, University College, Cardiff ; Gwen and Edgar Jones, Barry ; Dora Herbert Jones, Gregynog ; and Morgan James, Maesycwmmer. My niece, Mary McKenzie, prepared the street map from the Ordnance Survey. Mrs. Mary Berry and T. J. Lewis took the photographs. To Jenkin James and James Wardrop I am most grateful for seeing the little book through the press.

# CONTENTS

# ILLUSTRATIONS

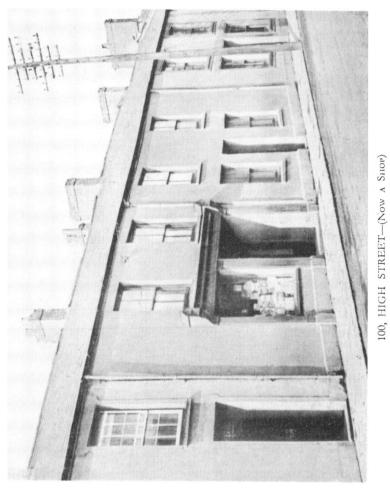

100, HIGH STREET—(Now a Shop)

# CHAPTER I

## THE MAGNETIC SOUTH, 1800-1870

| | | |
|---|---|---|
| Census 1801 Bedwellty Parish | ..... | 619 |
| Census 1841 Bedwellty Parish | ..... | 22,413 |

MY FIRST appearance was at Rhymney " in 100 High Street in September 1870 on Tuesday morning and was christened by Mr. Lewis of Newport at Brynhyfryd Chapel. Had the scarlet fever in April 1874 also his sister." So runs the entry in the large Family Bible. Had I been born a few miles further to the East or to the West, at Abergavenny or Aberdare for example, the rest of this chronicle would have been very different. Rhymney is a border village, partaking of England and Wales, and its dualism in space and in speech is an abiding element in the lives of all born within it. In 1870 it was not a century old. It was still new and growing ; in 1938 it looks back to its past and is far gone in decay. The iron works are in ruins, the coal pits are closed, and the brewery alone survives.

The village stands four and twenty miles from Cardiff at the head of a valley through which runs a river forming the boundary between Glamorgan and Monmouth. The river empties itself into the Bristol Channel at a point between Cardiff and Newport. The village near the source has been stabilized as Rhymney since the fifties, when the railway came ; the village near the mouth as Rumney. In the records from the opening of the twelfth century onwards the name undergoes many variations such as, Remni (Giraldus), Rymni, Reempni,

I

Rymhi, Rumney, Remney, Remeney and Remny (Leland, 1536), Rompney (Speed, 1610). Our less literate neighbours in Dowlais and Tredegar used to speak of going over to " the Rummy ", homonymous (to quote the *Times*) " with one of the mildest adjectives in old fashioned schoolboy slang." And in " Rummy Bridge " the names of two card games were united. Amateur philologists have displayed their usual ingenuity in explaining the word, associating it with Rimini, Rheims or Romney, and with meaning to divide, to extend, to embrace, a boundary, a marsh. The river was once a clear stream in a green valley. To call it a river is to flatter it. It was and is a thin trickle of water once pure turned into the colour of rust by limonite and by the offscourings of the brewery. Above the brewery in my boyhood we caught a species of minnow called *barabit* and there were a few pools in one of which the rite of baptism was publicly administered. But not even after heavy rains was there a long stretch of smooth surface, with deep water enough to cover the rocks and stones of the river bed completely. The irregular outlines of these obstacles were always visible and boys loved to squat above the flood on one of the big outcropping boulders.

The district lay off the beaten track of the eighteenth century explorers and tourists. There was neither country seat nor ecclesiastical ruin to be visited. The records of its pre-industrial life are therefore of the scantiest. Archdeacon Coxe travelling in the county in 1798 and 1799 admitted that the remoter parts had been seldom visited and never described.

" Under this head may be comprised the mountainous region watered by the Avon Lwyd, Ebwy, Sorwy, and Rumney; stretching from Pont y Pool to the frontiers of Brecknockshire and Glamorganshire, and comprehending nearly one fourth of the county. This region, though rich in minerals, is supposed to be barren of objects either interesting or picturesque, and is therefore called the Wilds of Monmouthshire, and seldom travelled by the gentry, except for the purpose of growse shooting. Impressed with the general prejudice, I neglected to explore it until my third tour."

Unfortunately for us the Archdeacon, even on his third tour, got no nearer Rhymney than Bedwellty where from the eminence of the white-washed parish church he surveyed "the rich vale of Carno." Nor is there anything helpful to be learned from the antiquarian pages of Leland and Camden or from the hardly less prosaic description of Monmouthshire in Thomas Churchyard's poem, *The Worthiness of Wales*.

In the years which followed the Conquest Normans and Welsh harassed each other continually on the Border and the *Chronicle of the Princes*, around 1070, speaks of fighting on the banks of the Rhymni. When a boy I followed its course towards its source to see the fossilized marks in the bed of the river of what one tradition described as the footprints of the Norman soldiers and their horses, and another as that of a horse ridden by the Blessed Mary (Mari Lwyd).

On old industrial maps of Rhymney two place-names are of interest. They are *Cae Twyn Fynachlog* and *Gwaun y Myneich*. The former was the name given to a monastery field in the neighbourhood of Pont Carno and the latter to the monks' moorland on which Rhymney Bridge station is situated. Dr. Birch in his *History of Margam Abbey*, states that a religious settlement attached to Margam was situated between the upper waters of the Rhymney and the Taff. The Cistercians of Margam owned land between Gelligaer and Fochriw. Fairs were generally held near monastic settlements and that of Twyn y Waun dates back to early times—to the twelfth century, according to some authorities. Twyn y Waun, 1,300 feet above sea level, was a focal point of the old Roman Road, the ridgeway from Cardiff to Brecon, and the old road from Merthyr to Abergavenny. Howel Harris preached here in 1766.

At the end of the eighteenth century there were a few sheep-farms on the hillsides, a few farm houses scattered along the water courses, the inhabitants living on the produce of the land, eggs and bacon, oatcake and vegetables. Much of the land then belonged to Benjamin Waddington of Llanover. The parish church of Bedwellty, St. Sannan's, stood a few miles down the valley on the eastern ridge, with a view of the Beacons and the Bristol Channel on a clear day. A little lower down, on the western ridge, stood the parish church of Gelligaer. And two or three miles still further down was Hengoed Baptist Church, founded in 1650, which played a dominant part in the theological controversies of the valley. During the Stuart persecutions members of the early nonconforming communities gathered by night for worship in remote farm houses in the Rhymney uplands. These retreats are now in ruins. The best known was Blaen Rhymni where dwelt Catherine Morgan. She was born in the third year of the reign of King James, lived under seven reigns, and died aged 106. She was 23 when her husband was born and she then made a promise that she would marry him when he reached manhood; she was 58 when he died in May, 1746, aged 35.

Through the long succession of seven silent centuries this region of woodland and rough pasture had remained unpeopled and untrodden except by a handful of peasants and shepherds from the day when William Fitz Osbern, Earl of

Hereford, fought the Welsh in 1070 almost down to 1794, when Catherine Morgan was interred in Vaynor churchyard, as recorded in the tablet above her resting place. The vast mineral riches beneath the surface lay undisturbed. A century later, when I was born in 1870, all was changed. The face of the hills was now scarred where men had scraped for iron-stone. The sides of the hills had been pierced and tunnelled and gutted for coal. Blast furnaces, steel works, company shops, Anglican churches and dissenting chapels, brewery and public houses, had appeared on the scene. The counties of Glamorgan and Monmouth had become the magnetic south into which multitudes of men, women and children had been drawn from north and mid Wales, and from the west of England. They came from distant rural areas on foot and in carts ; they came as Christians and as pagans, thrifty and profligate, clean and dirty ; and gradually sorted themselves in their new sur-roundings according to tradition and habit. Street criers went through Irish villages proclaiming that workmen were needed in South Wales to build railways and that they could earn four shillings a day. Empty coal boats returning from southern Ireland brought back hordes of labourers, whose passages were paid for out of money collected in England to relieve the famine. The empty valley was turned into a long trough full of human beings bustling and jostling each other for food and drink. For perhaps two thirds of the nineteenth century the Welsh element was dominant, but with the coming of the Board Schools in 1870 its influence was steadily undermined.

## II

The half century between 1760 and 1810 witnessed the foundation of the great change. During this half century, according to the county historians, oxen were still used for ploughing, game abounded in the valleys, a few goats survived of the herds which had cleared the mountain tops and moorlands of the scrub of birch and ash. The natives wore red or white flannel shirts, homespun blue cloth breeches and coats, with brass buttons. Red flannel was then, as in my youth, regarded as a prophylactic against colds. The women wore large chip hats trimmed with black silk and fastened under the chin. This was my grandmother's headgear seventy years later; and when going a journey arrayed in her best gown she used to turn it up over the hips and tuck it in at the waist, thus displaying a striped flannel petticoat.

Three events happened around 1760: Abraham Darby's discovery of how to make cast iron with coke in a high furnace; Smeaton's improved blast engine, which superseded the crude wooden and leather bellows; and the steam engine. All these combined to give the iron industry a great impetus. Three miles west of Rhymney, in 1759, Gentlemen of Glamorgan and Esquires of Bristol and others, nine in all, entered into a co-partnership " in the Art, Trade, Misterry and Business of the Iron Trade," for the establishment of a furnace for making pig iron. This was the beginning of the Dowlais Iron Works. Along the strip of mountain land which stretches for about eighteen miles from Hirwain to Blaenavon, advantage was taken of the presence together of coal, ironstone and limestone, to build furnaces which then became the foci of well-known iron works.

The first furnace in Tredegar, just over the hill from Rhymney, dates from 1764, but it must have been a small affair for the first census, that of 1801, showed a population of only 619 persons in the whole parish of Bedwellty, which included what there then was of Rhymney and Tredegar. The industries of Ebbw Vale, then a hamlet consisting of 36 houses, date from 1780. At Nantyglo, Sirhowy, Beaufort, Blaenavon, furnaces and forges for smelting and forging iron ore were erected in the closing years of the century.

Great difficulty was experienced in bringing blast engines from Neath Abbey to the new iron works. They were first brought to Newport, then to Abergavenny, and finally by horse-head over the mountains. There was an old track from Tredegar to Merthyr through Rhymney Bridge along which mules conveyed metal until puddling started in Tredegar itself in 1807.

Transport was inevitably a major problem in this precipitous region. Such main roads as there were had been assigned to the early Turnpike Trusts. In the first half of the eighteenth century their exactions were so oppressive that revolts were frequent and Parliament imposed the death penalty for the removal of a turnpike. To avoid their tolls hills and valleys had been traversed by straight and dangerous tracks regardless of gradients. In 1792 the local ironmasters promoted a bill for the construction of canals, railways and stone roads in the counties of Brecknock and Monmouth. "We are all canal mad," wrote a contemporary. In the following year the Turnpike Trustees of Monmouth obtained a further act which laid down a new set of tolls.

For every horse, mare, gelding, mule, ass, bull, ox, bullock, or other beast of draught, drawing any waggon—

not having the sole or bottom of the fellies of the wheels of the breadth of six inches the sum of fourpence halfpenny. For every coach (except stage coaches), berlin, landau, chariot, chaise, calash, chair, caravan, hearse or litter drawn by one horse, or other beast only, threepence.

This comprehensive list was presumably drawn up by a clerk in Whitehall who had never ventured further from Hyde Park than Hampstead Heath. And the exemptions from tolls in these early acts are not less interesting : coaches belonging to the Royal Family, to churchgoers, voters, and mourners ; posthorses carrying the mail, horses or carts of soldiers carrying their baggage, horses or carts carrying vagrants.

Although the tolls at each gate were thus limited by Parliament, there was no limit to the number of gates which could be placed on a road and it was this abuse which led to the Rebecca Riots in South Wales in the eighteen-forties (Genesis xxiv, 60). A Royal Commission followed and the roads were placed under County Boards and later under County Councils. But this is to anticipate.

The canal proprietors found waterway transit difficult and dilatory owing to the numerous locks and they constructed tramroads to link the works, the canals, and the seaports. Gradually the whole mineral area was threaded with these, on which ran waggons carrying about two and a half tons apiece. " Four tolerable horses " would draw twenty tons of iron from Tredegar to Newport in one day, a distance of twenty-three miles. The canal dock was brought into use in Newport in 1812. The railway " madness " was to follow thirty years later and in 1843 we find " A Constant Reader " writing to the *Monmouthshire Merlin* : " There is nothing like your mule for slow movement and dogged obstinacy save a body of canal proprietors."

But we are again anticipating and must return to Rhymney and watch the beginnings of its industries. The industrial history of Rhymney begins with the foundation of the first furnace in February, 1800. The accounts for labour, timber, stones, gunpowder, and for bills drawn on London still survive. By the fifth of June, 1801, the furnace was ready for filling with coke, by the thirteenth it was full. On the fourteenth (Sunday), at 7 p.m. communication pipes arrived from Neath. The entries throb with mounting excitement.

> 21st June (Sunday) Got engine ready at 8 p.m. Tried her found her all right put in Dam and began to blow ¼ before 3 o'clock on Monday morning. Seeing the water likely to be short kept 40 men making a weir across the river.

> 22nd June (Monday) H. T. Williams had his head bruised with riding on Engine Beam died at 12 o'clock at night.

> 23rd June (Tuesday) Cast for the first time 7 o'clock p.m. White Iron.

On " October 5th Mr. Murdock called examined Engine and found all right." This was probably the famous engineer and associate of Boulton and Watt.

> 26th Nov. (Thursday) At 4 o'clock began to blow Cupola. The engine quite sufficient for Furnace, Finery and Cupola.

> 27th Nov. (Friday) 3 o'clock a.m. Heavy snow and blowing hard. Stopt coal road. Stopt finery being short of coke and reduced blast on furnace.

> 28th Nov. (Saturday) At 2 o'clock a.m. had 60 men to open coal road finished by 6 o'clock a.m. Got down 84 trams of coal 63 tons began finery again.

29th Nov. (Sunday) 10 o'clock.   Snow storm all night.

30th Nov. (Monday) Roads stopt again.

Such were the birth pangs of the new works at the opening of the new century.   Born in a snowstorm they survived it and many another which followed in the next ninety years and at last succumbed to an economic blizzard.   The stones of the Old Furnace were pulled down in 1902 and built into some new dwelling houses.

The first ironmasters in South Wales were usually Englishmen. They are sometimes described in prospectuses as gentlemen, sometimes as capitalists, sometimes as esquires, and sometimes as grocers and teamen.   From John Lloyd's *Early History of the Old South Wales Iron Works* we learn that a Thomas Williams, one of the founders of the Old Furnace in Upper Rhymney, was one of the first South Wales men to take part or share in the promotion of the new iron works.   Another partner in the Rhymney venture was Richard Cunningham, who was also the manager.   Richard Crawshay of Cyfarthfa coveted the little works and in 1803 he entered into a fresh partnership with Williams and Cunningham, with his son-in-law Benjamin Hall, and with Watkin George, and together they formed The Union Iron Works Co. with a capital of £29,000.   This, John Lloyd thinks, included the cost of the new blast furnaces built at a point lower down the river, where the large Works were finally placed.   Richard Crawshay and Richard Cunningham soon quarrelled, the Cyfarthfa proprietor accusing the manager of being a swindler and threatening him with the County Gaol at Cardiff.   The works passed on the death of Richard Crawshay in 1810 to Benjamin Hall.   His son in turn was the Benjamin Hall after whom ' Big Ben ' is named.   He was chief Commissioner of Works in Lord Aberdeen's government and he established the Metropolitan Board of Works. He married the heiress of the Waddingtons of Llanover and became the first Baron of that name, while she was to become famous as Gwenynen Gwent (the Monmouth Bee), an enthusiastic patroness of all things Welsh.

Mr. Hall, senior, died at the early age of 39. One of his managers had been a Richard Johnson, who deserves to be honoured as the projector of what was then, and still is, called Newtown, near Rhymney Bridge, for the accommodation of the workpeople. The square three-storied houses were solidly built of trimmed stone, with spacious rooms and windows, and wide eaves. The width between the rows was that of a modern arterial road. But he died before his scheme was fully carried out.

On June 30th, 1824, the *Morning Herald* announced the forthcoming sale of "the Rumney Estate, late the property of Benjamin Hall Esq. whereon iron works have for many years been carried on under the firm of the Union Iron Co." The estate was taken over by a joint stock company, Forman and Co.

About this time (1825) furnaces known as the Bute Works were erected on land, on the Glamorgan side of the river, belonging to the Marquis of Bute, and opposite to the works of the Union Company. The design of these furnaces was so unusual as to attract widespread notice and drawings of them were hung in the Royal Academy. "The style was the Egyptian, and was adapted from the most striking part of the ruins of Dandyra, in Upper Egypt."

From the middle of the eighteenth century leases had been granted by Viscount Windsor, Lord of the Manor of Senghenith, Supra and Subtus, permitting this man and that to dig and

get coal and iron mine for fixed rents (not royalties) in and
around Rhymney. The 'patches' became known by the
names of the miners who 'scoured' them.

"The water having been panned up in the brook
or in the pond to form a head of water, and the mixture
of earth and iron ore being placed below, on the dam being
opened the strong rush of water cleansed the heavier ore
from the loose earth and clay, which latter were carried
down the brook to the sea. It saved much labour and the
ore was at once clean and fit for being sent to and used
in the furnaces."

The natural soil was washed away and this explains the
sterility of much of the land between Dowlais and Brynmawr.
More and more as the nineteenth century advanced, levels
and pits were opened and worked on the Bute and on the
Rhymney sides of the valley, some for coal, some for iron ore,
some for both. Many of them were Balance Pits, i.e., there
was a tank to hold water under each of the two cradles. The
tank under the empty cradle was filled at the top of the pit with
water to balance the cradle laden with mineral at the bottom.
When it descended to the bottom the water was emptied and
the cradle filled again with mineral. In order to avoid the
expense of raising the enormous quantities of water used to
operate the balance pits a water level was constructed which
connected a number of pits and conveyed the water from all
of these and discharged it into the river.

There were three shafts on the mountain on the Dowlais
side of the valley through which air was drawn to the levels
and pits and one of the flues still stands out prominently on
the hillside near Roger Pit. Sometimes rails were used as
guides for the ascending and descending cradles and they were

suspended by chains and rods in the old balance pits before steel ropes came to be used.  Many of the pits were troubled with flooding and the pumping engine had to be kept working day and night.  One of my boyhood memories is the rhythmic sighing of the pumping engine as the crank rose and fell, rose and fell, all through the night.

It was a land whose stones were iron.  Men were employed boring and blasting on the hillsides and the shale between the seams was baked into bricks if not too brittle.  The ironstone was piled into heaps by women, and after exposure to the air for the purpose of loosening, was put into the furnaces to be burnt with limestone and then run out into pig.  There was a brisk demand for lime wherewith to whitewash dwelling houses, stables, cowsheds, pig styes, hen coops, and the sheds in which coal was stored.

### III

The year 1831 was as depressing in the realm of business as 1931.  The numerous railways then in contemplation had led to many bubble schemes of over-production.  Large quantities of capital were embarked in fresh iron works :   new furnaces arose in all directions at the prospect of high prices.  A few princely fortunes were rapidly made.  Production out-ran demand ; prices fell.  Bar iron which fetched £19 10s. in 1800 was selling in 1831 at £5 per ton and even less.  It was a story of boom and slump, costly and cruel, to be frequently repeated throughout the century.

After the Rhymney Works had passed through various ups and downs a new company was formed in 1835 and constituted by deed of settlement in 1837 with a capital of £500,000

in 10,000 shares of £50 each. Its chairman was the Right
Hon. the Lord Mayor of London, William T. Copeland, M.P.
This company absorbed the Bute Iron Works from the Marquis
of Bute and was known as the Rhymney Iron Company. The
company on 24th March, 1871, was incorporated by registration
under the Companies Acts, 1862 and 1867, as a company limited
by shares and having a capital of £650,000. It in turn was
swallowed by the Powell Duffryn Co. in 1921.

The formation of the Rhymney Iron Company in the
thirties led to great local activity and a rapid rise in population.
Most of the streets were built in the next twenty years. The
High Street forms the back bone of the village and runs almost
as one thoroughfare from Twyn Carno at one end to Pontlottyn,
the next village, at the other. Carno Shop, then and today
a private business, had long been in existence. The year 1839
saw the building of the main or Lawn Company Shop, the
Brewery, and the Parish Church—all of them solid spacious
structures echoing what was called the ' Scotch style ' of the
houses at Newtown, and destined in the next half century to
be the most influential factors in the life of the village.

The moving spirit in all this activity was Andrew Buchan,
a Scot, trained as a carpenter, who had been employed at Abertysswg farm, and then had been engaged as a contractor to
divert the course and deepen the bed of the river so as to make
room for the erection of the Bute furnaces and diminish the
risk of floods. For this enterprise he had employed Irish
labourers who lived mainly on potatoes and herring. Their
presence led to rioting and soldiers were quartered in huts to
keep the peace. Hence, perhaps, the Barracks Road. To provide
for the needs of the navvies Andrew Buchan gave them notes
or orders on Carno shop for small amounts of groceries which

CARNO SHOP TO-DAY

Edwards, the proprietor, supplied in kind, obtaining the cash later from Buchan. This was the local beginning of the truck system. A counter-book used at Carno shop shows that an assistant on Friday, March 1st, 1839, served 106 customers to the amount of £30 11s. 4d., and on Saturday 94 customers to a total of £26 6s. 6d. Here is a list of prices charged per pound : butter 1s., sugar 8½d., tea 6s. and 7s., cheese 9d.: mutton 8d., liver 10d., bacon 10d., candles 8d., rice 4d., onions 3d., raisins 8d., bar soap 7d. ; flour was 3s. 4d. a stone, potatoes 8d. a stone, vinegar 3d. a pint ; snuff 8d. an ounce was sold in pennyworths, so was salt. Edwards, who was a native of Llanuwchllyn, turned his mind from the counter to the pulpit and was about to be ordained as a minister in Sirhowy when he died suddenly and was buried on the day fixed for his ordination. This was in 1835. Buchan took over the business. On December 31st, 1836, three of the directors of the new company, all of Laurence Pountney Hill in the City of London, and two of them Aldermen, entered into an agreement with Andrew Buchan appointing him to manage the new shop in middle Rhymney which " they had determined to open for the convenience of their workpeople." The manager was to be entitled to one fourth of the profits, such profits being guaranteed to amount to not less than £200 during each year. The company were to advance the capital required for the business at 5 per cent. and the business was to be conducted by Andrew Buchan and everything necessary to be done was to be done in his name only. He was not to buy or sell on credit without the knowledge and consent of the directors. With the erection of the brewery in 1839 Andrew Buchan became its manager also. At the meeting of the company on 7th February, 1838, the chairman's recommendation that a brew house for the supply of beer to all persons employed in the works should be built was approved and a month later a cheque for drawings was paid to an architect. In May a clerk was engaged from Aberdeen at a salary of £40 plus board and lodgings and in January of the following year tenders for coppers, etc., for £2,255 were accepted from Messrs. Pontifex. The brewery continues to do business with this firm a century later.

Until his death in 1870 Buchan was Rhymney's most conspicuous citizen and 'character'. He made valiant if unsuccessful attempts to master the Welsh language. He used to tease the girls by flicking snuff in their faces and then he would toss a coin to them by way of atonement. He would reward each player of the cricket team with a gold sovereign when it proved victorious. It was little wonder that his funeral procession was the largest ever seen in Rhymney. A brother David took £27,000 of Andrew's fortune to America. David's daughter's husband speculated in timber and lost it.

At their annual meeting in 1838, the company directors reported that " with the view to promote an object, not less their duty than their interest," and " because they had located on what were before almost barren mountains a population of 8,000 souls and that number was increasing daily," they were upon every principle, moral and religious, bound to provide and endow a church for the use of their tenants and others.

But they had not reckoned with the opposition of two dissenting individuals among the proprietary, the holders of 15 out of 10,000 shares. In vain did the *Glamorgan Gazette* urge upon the two objectors that the church would prove a remunerative investment and that the elevation of the moral character of the workmen would show itself in greater pecuniary profits. The *Mining Journal* also argued that labourers were useful and might be made respectable members of society, if means were taken for their instruction. One of the protesting shareholders sought an injunction from the Vice-Chancellor's Court to restrain the company. Mr. Knight Bruce, for the plaintiff, urged the Court not to act upon the detestable principle that the end justified the means. The successors of the directors next year might be Jews, who upon the same principle might apply £4,000 to the building of a synagogue. His Honour the Judge refused the injunction, probably because it was discovered that the company in the meantime had petitioned Parliament for leave to bring in a bill for the purpose of building a church and schools. When it came before the Honourable Members, Mr. Baines said that he was reluctant to divide the House but where was it to stop ? If a church this year, it might be a chapel next year, and then perhaps a theatre. The Third Reading passed by seventy-one to eight. So Rhymney got its first church. Its only peculiarity is that its altar and chancel are in the West and not in the East. Its bells were cast in London in 1875 by John Warner and Sons.

Long before this religious services had been held in the Long Room of the Rhymney Inn, near the Old Furnace, a sermon or school at nine o'clock on Sunday mornings by the Protestants and at eleven by the Papists. This latter service was attended by a detachment of soldiers from the Dowlais barracks where they were retained at the wish of Sir John Guest, M.P.

The first ironmasters were men of energy and resource, rough and domineering, hard and avaricious. They took great risks and sometimes lost all. The second and third generations usually had these qualities much diluted ; they had less initiative, more tolerance, softer manners, but their sense of ownership was strengthened not weakened by the flux of time.

What is said of the Krupps, father and son, could easily be paralleled in the history of the families of the Welsh ironmasters and coalowners. "In contrast to his father, the powerful, strong-willed, harsh and four-square founder of the gigantic firm, a man born to rule, Alfred Krupp was a delicate man, sensitive, nervous, tender hearted."

The early ironmasters did not always feel themselves very secure. Beneath the surface there was much discontent with their rule which was later to manifest itself as Chartism. At Nantyglo Joseph and Crawshay Bailey had built and provisioned a fortress into which they might escape in the hour of danger. Three hundred Chartists marched past the Old Furnace on their way from Dowlais to Newport on November 3rd, 1839. What part the men and women of Rhymney played in the rising I have not been able to discover. Secrecy was essential and what most impressed the inspector sent by the Government to report on the state of education, was "the unusual phenomenon—of large masses of the working population capable of continuing and keeping secret from the magistrates and everyone in authority, until the moment of execution, a well-organized plan for a combined attack upon a populous town distant from nine to eighteen miles from their habitations in the hill country."

## IV

But these "colonies in the desert," as the mining villages were labelled by the inspector, were not entirely cut off from the outside world. He himself found a local bookseller in one of them who sold eight copies of *Chambers Journal* and eight of the *Penny Magazine*. And he found three catalogues of Welsh books, comprising 720 items, all but 114 of them devoted to religious subjects.

We have seen that from the days of the Stuarts men from lower down the valley had met secretly for worship and the celebration of the sacraments in farm houses hidden in pockets of the plateau above Rhymney. These gatherings continued after the danger of persecution had ceased. With the beginnings of the iron works, at the turn of the century, the various denominations met in private houses. The first chapel, now Ebenezer, Twyn Carno, dates from 1807. Others followed. These early chapels were small halls, measuring about thirty by twenty feet, with a pulpit and a few large pews but no gallery. They were extended repeatedly with the growth of the population, and rebuilding involved their members in a perpetual struggle to pay for them, a struggle from which the endowed Church of England was exempt. In the late forties, during a period of bad trade, the unpaid builder of Jerusalem Chapel locked it up and kept the key. This forced the minister to hold meetings in his own house and a communion service in his garden. Somehow he contrived to enter the chapel and there he remained night and day for about a week, food being brought to him by his friends. The chapel was put up to auction on two occasions before it was finally restored to the congregation by the generous action of a neighbouring church.

The early nonconformist pastors lived upon the alms of their congregations and were paid fifteen or twenty shillings a week with house and coal. They were the natural leaders of the people and among them were to be found men of unusual gifts of mind and character. The chapels were schools of adult education and cradles of democracy where men and women learned to govern themselves by trial and error. The conduct of these early societies is marred by what seems to us today gross vulgarity and endless disputation. Each sect had its own doctrine and dialect and behaviour. The Wesleyans were not very numerous; they kept to themselves, and their ministers used a stilted Welsh vocabulary. It will, I think, be agreed that the ministers of the Calvinistic Methodists were the best educated in Wales and perhaps for this reason they were called Big Heads. They were apt to be conservative and austere and a trifle more Pharisaic than their neighbours.

They disciplined any member suspected of being mixed up in the riotous proceedings of the Chartists or in the mysteries of the trade unions. This pleased the employers and at the time of the Chartist trouble Sir John Guest sent a cheque of £50 to a Dowlais chapel with a letter commending its sense and its religion. In Rhymney the weakness of the Baptists was intemperance, but, as Burke might say, you cannot draw up an indictment against a whole denomination on the behaviour of two or three chapels. The early records report not only large additions to the membership of the churches but numerous losses through offences against the standard of conduct laid down. The diaconate acted as a tribunal. The offenders formed a fluctuating margin of feeble brethren who found the temptations of Pay Saturday too much for them but were unwilling to backslide entirely into 'the World' and renounce all public profession of religion. Some contrived to tipple in secret and to retain their church membership and although suspicion might rest upon them evidence might not be forthcoming to justify their expulsion. Drinking was encouraged by the practice of paying the master-miner or contractor in notes or gold; these he exchanged at a public house and paid the workmen their wages there. In Rhymney this practice continued into the seventies, but as far back as 1840 Dowlais Iron Company arranged " at considerable expense " for a sufficient supply of gold, silver and copper coins for the payment of their workmen separately.

The serpent of dissension was a frequent visitor in the garden of religious life. There were not a few ' split chapels ' but the fissiparous tendencies of the congregations were at least proof of vitality and evidence that there were subjects deemed to be worth fighting about. Fighting there certainly was, the most famous local battle being on the subject of baptism. This was in 1841 and lasted two days in the open air in front of two chapels. Challenges had been issued and accepted and two ministers had been chosen to put the case for the Sprinklers and the Dippers respectively : John Jones for the former and T. G. Jones for the latter. The Baptists were charged with spreading damaging rumours in advance about Mr. John Jones, calling him an ungodly man, an infidel, a monster from Llangollen. Scurrilous and anonymous leaflets were pushed by night under doors and malicious paraphrases of biblical passages were pasted on the door of the Congregational chapel. Feeling ran high as November 1st approached and on that morning the roads for many miles around were alive with men and women tramping to the scene of the debate. Estimates of the number present varied from fourteen to twenty thousand, including sixty-four ministers. Rules of debate were settled. Only baptism was to be debated ; each side was to speak alternately for seven minutes ; only the two champions were to speak and they were not to appeal to the audience for support ; no obstacle was to be put in the way of the speakers and the audience was to keep silent during the proceedings ; two chairmen were to preside, one for each party. All the rules were soon broken. At one point a part of the stage gave way. At another one leader called the other "Tom Paine, Deist". This led to great commotion and the crowd pressed forward towards the platform shouting for twenty minutes, and the insulted champion was carried away on a chair by his supporters. Throughout the debate biblical texts were bandied about in Welsh and in Greek. "But that is the genitive case?" shouted one. "No, it is the accusative case," retorted the other. "The two are debating so badly that we ought to choose two others," interjected the chairman. Another advised the audience to study their Testament quietly at home.

It was a sorry exhibition and it ended in complete confusion. Both sides claimed a victory and for months after the parties continued to libel each other in the press and in pamphlets. The experiment was never repeated and few today in Rhymney have even heard of the Baptist Fair.


## V


From the earliest days there had been small "private adventure" schools held in the houses of the teachers, and occasionally ministers taught elementary classes in the chapels. But forty years after the founding of the first furnace, there were in the whole parish of Bedwellty, with its population of twenty thousand, only 825 children attending the common day and dame schools. Fees ranged from three pence to eight pence per week. The inspector discovered piles of detached book covers and leaves too black for further use, " betokening the result of long struggles with unmeaning rows of spelling, with confinement and constrained positions, and the other adversities of elementary learning." This was in 1839.

In 1847 the records show that a school was located in Twyn Carno chapel under the auspices of the four nonconformist denominations and that it was attended by 114 children classified as follows : Latter Day Saints 1, Church of England 13, Baptists 18, Wesleyans 18, Independents 28, Calvinistic Methodists 36. The headmaster received a salary of £13 17s. per month. The school pence paid from 6th September, 1847, to 21st August, 1848, amounted to £33 5s. 7d. ; books and slates cost for the same period £2 5s. 11d., and the master's travelling expenses to Rhymney were £1. To balance matters the committee had to collect about £20 over the year.

The publication at this time of the reports of commissioners sent to investigate the state of education in the Principality led to steps being taken in Rhymney to provide a British School. An account of this attempt at denominational co-operation, written on odd scraps of paper and preserved by the descendants of the secretary, the Rev. George Owen, illustrate some of the difficulties which had to be surmounted. Should there be two schools, each on one floor, one for the upper and one for the lower end of the village ? John Evans offered to build the two separate schools for £600 ; John Prothero offered to build one school on two floors for the same sum in Upper Rhymney. The Baptists wanted the former arrangement, the Methodists and Congregationalists the latter and they won. The Baptists thereupon withdrew from the scheme and the remaining two denominations had to shoulder the burden for many years. Here is a copy of the contract entered into with John Prothero.

At a meeting of the Cambrian Day School held in the School Room Twyn Carno July 11.

It was proposed seconded and carried by the Meeting that John Prothero carpenter should have the building of the new School Room on the following conditions.

That after the building is completed he shall bring in his bill of particulars and if the committee should think it too much they may choose two competent persons to value it and if they value it less than his bill he is willing to stand to the loss and if they value it more he will not require the addition, the size of the timbers to be according to Mr. Evan Williams.

The length of the building to be 57 feet and breadth 30 feet hight 20 feet from the floor to the square.

David Richards in the chair.

Rules for the conduct of the enterprise were drawn up. The members of the governing body must believe the cardinal doctrines of the evangelical faith; the children had to be over five years of age and members of a Sunday School; the master had to be a Welshman, a Christian, and a member of one of the four nonconformist churches. The curriculum embraced Reading, Writing, Arithmetic (written and mental), Grammar, History, Geography, Astronomy and Mensuration. Nothing contrary to the Christian religion was to be taught.

Children came to the new school from Newtown in the north and Pontlottyn in the south and some fifteen years were to pass before the denominations got together again and put up a school at the lower end of the village. About this time also (1863), the Roman Catholics erected a school for 150 of their children.

In the meantime, in 1858, the Company provided a National School in Middle Rhymney at a cost of £3,000. It was on one floor, measuring 100 feet by 50 feet, and was much superior to the rival erections of the Dissenters. A part of it was set aside as a reading room to accommodate the Literary and Scientific Institution established in 1850. This was managed by the leading officials of the Company and the ministers of religion. Workmen paid 1s. a quarter and all other than workmen 1s. 6d. Funds were added to by means of lectures and concerts. The Institution opened with 126 members and with loans and gifts of books. The list of these opens with

Thiers *Consulate and Empire* 10 Parts.
Goldsmith *Animated Nature* 2 Volumes.

Mr. Trump follows with the loan of Plutarch's *Lives*, Byron, and Washington Irving's *Bracebridge Hall* and the firm of Chambers figures with *Information, Miscellany, Papers for the People* and *Edinburgh Journal.* In Welsh I find a gift of the *Traethodydd*, the *Gwladgarwr*, the *Eurgrawn*, and a translation of the works of Josephus. Books were bought from Sotheran's— Sotheran, Son and Draper as the firm then was, in Eastcheap— at a discount of twenty per cent. Here are a few items from bills in the middle fifties : Thierry's *Norman Conquest,* Curzon's *Monasteries,* Thackeray's *Lectures,* Gilfillan's *Bards,* Gibbon's *Rome,* Edgeworth's *Tales,* Herschell's *Light,* Brewster's *Magnetism,* Ruff's *Guide,* many novels by G. P. R. James, Charles Lever, and Bulwer Lytton. At the foot of one of the bills it is stated that the *History of the Covenanters* is "not known" and that "it is necessary to order Draper's *Organisation of Plants* from America. Shall we do so?" One famous book has an invoice all to itself, dated Dec. 17, 1855 :

Macaulay's *England*, vols. 3 & 4 36s.     £1  9  0
                        Postage     £     1 10
                                        ─────────
                                        £1 10 10

Thirty years later I read many of these books, none, I confess, of the scientific works. I honour the memory of that early committee, Richard Johnson, Henry Trump, Jenkin Matthews, Richard Bedlington, Owen Rogers, and the rest, who filled the shelves for me with so catholic a selection. Did the public of their day make good use of the Library ? I open at random a page of the issuing book and this is what I find on four consecutive days :

*Recollections of a Gaol Chaplain.*
*Ben Brace* (Capt. Chamier)
*The Bivouac* (Maxwell).
*Decision of Character* (Foster).
*County Curate* (Gleig).
*The Girondists* (Lamartine).
*Vicar of Wrexhill* (Mrs. Trollope)
*Oliver Twist* (Dickens).
*The Poacher* (Marryat).
*Rattlin the Reefer* (Howard).
*The Buccaneers* (Mrs. S. C. Hall).
*Jacqueline of Holland* (Grattan).
*Nineveh and its Remains* (Layard).
*Natural Philosophy* (Herschell).
*Rienzi* (Lytton).
*Nineveh* (2 vols.) (Layard).
*Chronicles of Crusaders.*
*Zohrab* (Morier).
*Thaddeus of Warsaw* (Miss Porter).
*Peter Simple* (Marryat).

One comment suggests itself in looking at this list—the number of authors who profited by being in the employment of the State. Chamier and Marryat and Howard were captains in the Navy ; Gleig was Chaplain-General of the Forces, Layard a diplomatist, Morier a secretary to an Ambassador, and Lytton a statesman. A sample month shows 170 books issued and of these only forty-five were fiction. The first printed catalogue which I possess (1860) shows a total of 749 volumes and of these 279 were classified as Novels and Tales.

When the School Board took over the Middle School in the seventies the Library was moved to Tre York House, the Company continuing to give rent, coal and light free until 1914. But the great mass of the workmen remained unreached until 1894, when a public meeting of miners was convened and 600 of them decided to make regular subscriptions through the Company's pay offices to the support of the Library. In 1905 a new Institute was built at a cost of £3,000 and with a membership of 2,500 mainly employees of the Company. The money for this new building came from annual surpluses, an increased poundage on the workmen's wages, and loans from local residents at four and a half per cent. The stock of books rose to about 6,000 with a weekly issue around 300.

## VI

The years 1840-1860 may be regarded as enclosing the active promotion of railway communication in South Wales, carried out despite the opposition of canal proprietors and turnpike trustees. As far back as 1825 Crawshay and Joseph Bailey and Sir Charles Morgan, Bart. had obtained an Act for the construction of a railroad from Abertysswg, just below Rhymney, to Bassaleg where the new railway was to join the existing Sirhowy line to Newport. This Act had one admirable clause which ran :

III.  And be it further enacted that the furnace of every
Steam Engine....shall be constructed upon the Principle
of consuming its own Smoke.

These lines were converted into railways for the use of
locomotive engines and later were empowered to convey pas-
sengers.  In the forties and fifties Newport had been of more
consequence to us than Cardiff.  Its exports rivalled those
of Bristol and it was spoken of as an infant Liverpool.  But
this was changed for us in 1858 by the construction of a railway
connecting Rhymney with Cardiff and the exciting news that
from January 1st, 1859, three trains would run in each direction
daily between Cardiff (Adam Street) and Rhymney.  The fares
were 4s. 2d., 3s. 1d., and 2s., and the fastest time was 1 hour
17 minutes for the 24½ miles.  A day return ticket to Cardiff
on Saturdays cost 2s.  Today there are fourteen trains each
way and the fastest does the journey in an hour.  The fares
today for two classes are 5s. and 3s. ; day returns 4s. 9d., 3s. 2d.
Improved transport stimulated developments at the Works
and in 1862 the Plate Mill was built which afterwards became
known as the Steel Mill.  Plates of many widths and thicknesses,
including armoured plates for warships, were manufactured
up till 1868 when the mill was converted into a rail mill.  In the
early seventies the Bessemer process was discovered and by
1877 it had been adopted in Rhymney.  At this time six furnaces
and three cupolas were being used for the manufacture of steel.
Over the hill, at Dowlais, were the " largest steel works in
the world " with seventeen furnaces.  We had nineteen loco-
motive engines running to and fro.  Britain had become the
workshop of the world and Rhymney was a vigorous if modest
partner in the vast national effort.  We were on the threshold
of the expansion of manufacture in Germany and the United
States but we did not know this and another twenty one years

were to pass before their combined competition strangled us. We were also on the eve of two important developments in local government : the formation of a school board in 1871 which I shall touch on later, and of a local board under the powers of the Local Government Act of 1859. At the first election the officials of the Company—the manager of the Works, the cashier, and the manager of the Shop—were at the top of the poll, with a collier, a contractor, a grocer, and the Catholic priest, excluded at the bottom. The Board appointed a Surveyor, Collector and Inspector of Nuisances, all in one, at a salary of £2 per week and among its first resolutions was one for the scavenging of the town, the erection of ash bins and the selection of a site for depositing rubbish. This Local Board held its last meeting in December, 1894, and was succeeded by an Urban District Council. Four years later it had a Labour chairman and Justice of the Peace for the first time.

In 1870, in the issue of January 15th, the local correspondent of the chief Welsh newspaper, the *Baner*, summed up the life of the little village as he then saw it, and with his summary we may fitly conclude this review of 1800 to 1870.

"It is famous on many counts. To it belong many men who are gifted, industrious and energetic, poets, essayists, historians, and musicians worthy to stand on any platform with the chief musicians of Wales. There are fifteen handsome chapels for the worship of the true and living God, and many godly men gather within them. There are also to be found here hundreds of nonconformists, honest enthusiastic men of principle, full of zeal for every good cause. A standing evidence of their industry is the British School, splendid and convenient, erected in Twyncarno among its large and increasing population."

# CHAPTER II

*What is your name ? and your father's ? Your country ?
and where was your prowess ?*
    *Kasmylos : Euagoras : Pythian boxer : from Rhodes.*
                               SIMONIDES.

FOR a few guineas a commoner elevated to the House of Lords may employ the services of an heraldic expert who will trace his ancestry back to Charlemagne, and even further back for a few more guineas. We could pride ourselves in our village on one citizen only whose ancestry was of demonstrable distinction. He had inherited the splendid name of Scudamore and was thus a member of one of the most ancient families in England, one of whom, Sir John de Scudamore, had married Alice, daughter of Owen Glyndwr in 1396. But the Joneses, like the Basques, do not date. Unaided I have not been able to go beyond the Wars of Napoleon. And unlike Simonides I cannot pack the story into two lines.

Among the men drawn by the lure of ' the Works ' from West Wales was William Jones, once a soldier in the French Wars, then a tailor. He hailed from Pentre Cynwil in Carmarthenshire and one of his three wives was Esther Elias, a native of Blaenannerch, Cardiganshire. They settled in the upper part of Rhymney known as Twyncarno. Both were zealous Calvinistic Methodists and William Jones induced Sir Benjamin Hall to grant a plot of land on which to build the first Ebenezer Chapel in 1806 and in due course became

a deacon in this chapel.   At one time he is said to have employed
as many as nine assistants in his tailoring business.   One of them,
his son William, used to make my suits as a boy.   He came
to a bad end as will appear later.   Another son Samuel became
a deacon and so in 1860 became a third, Enoch.   These two
carried stones from the bed of the Rhymney river to build
the second Ebenezer in 1849.   It is with Enoch we are specially
concerned at this point of our narrative.   He was born on the
first of July, 1826, in a house near Ebenezer Chapel and was
given a better education than was then customary, going first
to a dame's school, kept by Mrs. Blackmore, then to a ' private
adventure ' school kept by ' John Evans—One   Arm ', and
thirdly to an ' educational establishment ' at Cefn-Coed-Cymmer
for a ' quarter of schooling ' where he received the finishing
touches.   The youthful Enoch was then sent to work in the
iron ore mines at Roger's Pit and here he remained for seven
years with the exception of a few months, during a strike, when
he worked at Sirhowy.   During this period he seems to have
backslided from chapel into the ' World '.   He is next seen,
aged twenty, as a clerk in the stores of the Rhymney Iron Company—the centre for the supply of the needs of the various
departments :   the blacksmith's shop, the fitting shop, the
pattern shop, the foundry and so forth.   Here in due course
he became the chief storekeeper and served the Company forty-
seven years in all.

Meanwhile in the village of Clutton in Somerset there
had been born in 1788, Job Cook, and in 1807, when he was
19 and a collier he married Martha Carter by banns in the parish
church.   Her father was gamekeeper to a local squire.   Neither
Job nor Martha could write and each marked the register with
a cross, but the three witnesses George and Artulus Cook and

EBENEZER CHAPEL

AND BIRTHPLACE OF ENOCH JONES IN FOREGROUND

Robert Carter signed their names. Job became a local preacher with the Wesleyans and underground manager of Frysbottom Pit, on the outskirts of Clutton, and the young couple lived in one of the two cottages which still stand near the fence which marks the site of the old disused shaft. The other was occupied by the timekeeper.

Eight miles down the valley from Rhymney beyond Pengam, is Fleur-de-lys, familiarly called " The Flower ". Two explanations of the name are given : one that it is due to a colony of Frenchmen who started spelter works near the New Inn ; the other, that a Mr. Moggeridge named the place after a visit to France, discovering some similarity between the place where he stayed in France and the land he owned near Pengam. Be that as it may, lured by " the Works " from Somersetshire, Job Cook in the thirties settled as a gaffer at Pennar Colliery, Pentwynmawr, near Crumlin, bringing with him his wife Martha and four of his ten children : Mercy, Andrew, Martha and Harriet. Job and his wife moved to " The Flower ", Mercy remained at Crumlin and married, Martha died, Andrew went to America, and Harriet went into domestic service in Rhymney, where she met and married Enoch Jones, English and Welsh uniting. They settled in Rhymney. Enoch was then earning eleven shillings a week. Eight children were born to them and one of them Mary Ann, was my mother.

In the bosom of the shire of Cardigan nestles Llangeitho, a tiny hamlet famous in religious annals and a place of pilgrimage to a Welsh Methodist much as Canterbury is to an Anglican. Here in a wayside cottage, called Gwynfil, two rooms downstairs and one up, lived Benjamin Jones, familiarly known as Bennie Gwynfil, his wife and children. He was descended from a freeholder in the neighbouring Penuwch and was engaged in building cottages of earth and straw, called 'clom' in some parts of Wales.    Once on a visit to Llangeitho I asked whether Bennie a was good builder and received the following reply: "He could build with both hands, with his right if he were well paid, with his left if he were badly paid." Which reminds me of one of Bismarck's assistants at the Colonial Office in Berlin who wrote, "with his right or with his left hand just as his superiors wished." In the "season" Benjamin Jones travelled the shires as far as Hereford and Gloucester from farm to farm as groom with a stallion. The most famous of these was Comet I. There still survives in Cardiganshire a black leather collar adorned with fourteen brass shields recording the prizes won at shows by this splendid horse :

Aberaeron :  1861, 1864, 1865, 1866, 1870.

Aberystwyth :  1861.

Cardigan :  1864, 1865, 1866, 1870.

Carmarthen :  1868, 1870, 1871, 1872.

Comet II met with a tragic fate.  A man riding home in the dead of night was passing the Fedw farm and observed another man crossing the road stealthily near the farm.  His suspicions were aroused but he rode on, and only when he had reached the rising ground above Llangeitho Church did he halt and look back over the Vale of Aeron.  He then saw a fire raging.  He galloped back, roused some villagers and Enoch Morgan, the farmer, who reached the stable just in time to see his horse fall at his feet, burnt to death.  No motive for the crime is suggested in the records from which this account is taken.

Despite the ambiguous testimony to his building practice my inquiries show Benjamin Jones to have been a happy kindly and voluble individual with a genial temper which made him popular in the farms he visited, especially with the dairy-

ONE PENUEL ROW

maids. One contemporary summed him up to me as " a topper of a man." He had a son David Benjamin, born, according to the Family Bible, in Llangeitho "at two minutes past two o'clock Thursday, Association Day of the Methodists in August the ninth day of year 1844." This boy set out in his early teens to seek his fortune in the Eldorado of that day, " the Works ", travelling miles in a cart first to Merthyr and thence to Tredegar and finally to Rhymney where he found a job, lighting fires in the Company Shop. One morning, when engaged on his task, he found the feet of a burglar in the grate. The intruder had stuck fast during the night in his descent and had to be dug out. David Benjamin developed into a grocer's assistant in the business of Andrew Buchan and Co., the Andrew Buchan who managed the shops, the brewery, and the farm of the Rhymney Company. In due course he succeeded to the management of the shops and the farm but not the brewery and became known locally as D.B. Meanwhile Mary Ann, the daughter of " Enoch Jones the Stores " was working at her trade, the shaping of straw hats : the straw was of special quality and was used for several hats in turn. It was undone and resewn in new patterns on wooden blocks as the fashions changed. I recall large paper bags with " M. A. Jones, Straw Hat and Bonnet Manufacturer " printed on them and I regret the blocks were ultimately used for firewood and did not find their way to the National Museum.

David Benjamin and Mary Ann married each other in December, 1869, and they went to live at 100, High Street, in the centre of the main thoroughfare of the village, and Enoch and Harriet Jones moved from this house to a house owned by the Company, 1, Penuel Row, near Penuel, the Baptist Chapel. I possess only one of my father's letters to my mother before

their marriage.   He was twenty-four but was still finding difficulties in putting his passion into correct English.   My mother
was at Crumlin at the time, where some of the Cook family
lived.   Here is the letter :

RHYMNEY SHOP,<br>
Septr. 9th, 1868.

Dr. Polly,

   I am happy to inform you that I have received your
kind letter this morning and was very glad to here that
you were safe and that you are quite happy but I  have
not the least doupt less than you be much happier if I was
a long side of you with the arms of love guiding you and
a faithful heart to comfort thee.

   I have sent you a short note yesterday.   I hope you
have received it with the everlasting love to the one that write
it as his for ever and ever to you.   Last night no place
to go to put bed to comfort myself and soon as I got to
bed my mind was running over the mountains towards
the viaduck of Crumlyn and the heart of yours.   Somehow
it wouldnt sleep put it was telling me that the mind was
lonely and no moonlight to accompany us both.   Bed
by myself but after all my eyes was still with me so I have
nothing to do put try and look through the window and
there I was listening to hear if I could see something put
before long I could see the Bird in all colours come and
told me you have a friend and the last word she said tonight
after prayers was that she have a friend in Rhymney, has
a plant of love in his heart for which I wish you to comfort
him before dark and tell him the secret that I am his for ever.
I cannot tell you how I slept after that.   I hope you possess
such feelings, my dearest Polly.

BRYNHYFRYD CHAPEL

I am sure you are tired all ready of reading such folley but you must think at all times that the one that wrights it is always faithful and true. I havent been up the road since Sunday put I shall go tonight if possible. I havent no news to inform you put I see this week very long. I see it all ready almost as long as a week. I hope you do injoy yourself first class. I shall trust and hope that on Sunday before dinner I shall received your sweetly kiss and arms around my neck. So mind to write back. If you havent a letter everyday would welcome and great comfort to your true lover . . . " (rest of letter torn and undecipherable).

In 1861 Enoch Jones with three colleagues were directed by the mother church of Twyncarno to proceed to build and care for the new Calvinistic Methodist Chapel at the other end of the village, to be known as Brynhyfryd (Mount Pleasant). Enoch Jones kept all the building accounts, superintended the erection, and remained secretary of the church for thirty years. His handwriting was distinguished by the perfect formation of each letter and his list of church members in the ruled folios in which the accounts were kept would compare not unfavourably with the Rolls of Honour of post-war scribes. I was christened in Brynhyfryd the first of nine children of David Benjamin and Mary Ann Jones. My father was then earning 32s. per week and paying 5s. in rent to my grandfather who owned 100, High Street. But he bought all goods from the Company Shop at cost price and as the family grew in numbers this perquisite was increasingly important.

If it be true that a long pedigree ought to have broad possessions so that a sympathy may appear between the extraction and the estate, so small possessions should go with a short pedigree—a dictum illustrated by this chapter.

# CHAPTER III

## SCHOOL AND PLAY

*Mi welais rhyw Italian*
*Yn chwareu organ cul*
*A dwy lygoden ganddo*
*Yn dawnsio round i'r wheel.*

WILLIAM DAVIES, 1838.

I CAN take neither credit nor blame for my ancestry, nor can I explain why children born of the same stock and reared in not dissimilar, if not identical circumstances, show such wide divergence in adult life. Scientific research has thrown some light on the interdependence of psychical and somatic aspects of behaviour. In my youth we mingled manganese with ores to give toughness to steel. Today we are told that the maternal instinct varies with the presence or absence of manganese and that the tears of sorrow and the dry mouth of fear are illustrations of chemical processes.

There is no child in general, there are only children in particular, each endowed with a specific biological capital or equipment. When nine children in the same family appear to touch the same ribbon and to start from scratch, nature has in fact already settled the handicaps for life's Grand National. Environment will provide what to one are obstacles and to another opportunities along the course. One child falls a victim to meningitis in its second year, another to scarlet fever in its sixth, and so on to the end of the race.

Public policy proceeds on the assumption that systems of education can exploit and improve our original endowment. You cannot train a black currant into an apricot, to use Ruskin's illustration in *Modern Painters*. " The tender pride and sweet brightness of golden velvet " of one are beyond the reach of the other, but the currant has its own rounded perfection and modest bloom. Good gardening and sunshine may do much for both.

Chance, said Pasteur, favours the prepared mind. The task of preparation, the gardening process, which we call education began in my case formally at the Upper Rhymney School but before I went there I had been given a name at the christening ceremony to distinguish me from the rest of mankind. Welsh names of persons are notoriously limited in range and this poverty is in marked contrast with the variety and richness of Welsh place names, many of which unfold their beauty like a nature film :

> Llanarmon Dyffryn Ial
> Rhos Llanerch Rugog
> Llanerchymedd
> Pont Rhyd Fendigaid
> Llanfihangel Genau'r Glyn

English editors of the better sort pride themselves on the accuracy of their French, German, or Italian quotations and they take trouble to spell correctly the names of remote villages in China or Japan, but they seldom get these beautiful Welsh words right. Old makers of maps were great offenders. One of Black's *Guides* in the sixties turns Mynydd Islwyn into Mynydwssllwyd, and then adds the stupid comment that it is " a name which it is supposed beats any other proper name in Great Britain." Other English variants of this name which

I have noted are worth tabulating as examples of the ingenuity of ignorance :

| | |
|---|---|
| Monythusloin | Monethuslin |
| Monythusloine | Munithuslan |
| Monythusloyn | Mjunith Istloyne |
| Monythusloyne | Monithisloyn |

Prizes were awarded in the early Eisteddfods for essays on the inconsistency of putting English inscriptions on the tombstones of the Welsh and of giving extraneous names to their children, but the essays went unread or unheeded.

The poverty in respect of persons has been surmounted by various devices. By nicknames, for example. Here is an assortment from Rhymney : Johnnie Fresh Air, John One Suit, John Every Bit, Dai Goose, Mari'r Ochor Draw, Mary Jane Quavers (*a* pronounced as in cat), Evan Bolgi, Mrs. Williams Move About, and Enoch Brynbrith. Many Welsh preachers are never mentioned without the addition of the village to which they were attached : John Jones, Talysarn, John Williams, Brynsiencyn. Our local celebrities added the name of the county, Gwent (Monmouthshire), and we had amongst us Ioan, Gwilym, Ossian and Heman Gwent. The pseudonyms of bards and singers are usually inflated : they are lions, eagles, or nightingales, never frogs or sparrows. In the Victorian age it was the practice in naming children to search through the less familiar chapters of the Old and New Testaments. In my youth in Rhymney I remember little Welsh boys and girls, whose parents were so lacking in patriotism as to christen their children Obadiah, Zechariah, Zephaniah, Azariah, Keziah, Keturah, Israel, and Lazarus. In the event of a Nazi invasion of Wales these will be hard put to it to prove their Celtic origin. One Baptist minister who had an elementary knowledge of chemistry, boldly prefixed Darwin, Huxley and Tyndall to the Jones which his sons shared with so many of us. It was a later generation of parents' which turned from the Bible to the Mabinogion and other mediaeval sources for the graceful and courtly names which now variegate the list of graduands at each university degree ceremony. In the most enlightened homes the narrow provincialism of the Bible has given place to a rich cosmopolitanism in the choice of combinations prefixed to the inescapable Jones and Evans, Roberts and Williams. We may now delight in Eira Nansi Rosemary, Morfudd Priscilla, Alexandrina Myrtle.

There was some discussion as to whether I should be called Benjamin or Nicholas in addition to Thomas but there was no agreement between the paternal and maternal champions and I had to be content with one name, usually abbreviated, and make the best of it. In recent years, such is the desire to conserve energy in Whitehall, it has been still further shortened to the bare initials. I am clinging to my identity by my two eyelashes so to speak. When I went to school there had been eight Tom Joneses on the register but the fifth place was vacant and I became Tom Jones Five and to my remaining contemporaries in Rhymney that is what I am still when I visit them. If only my parents had stuck in an ' h ' and made me Johnes, like the founder of the Hafod Press, I should have attained uniqueness and distinction at once.

Years later when I was taking a degree in Glasgow and my father and mother had come up for the capping ceremony, my father saw in a shop window a book called *The History of Tom Jones* by Henry Fielding. He was intrigued and went in and bought it for eighteen pence vowing he would read it. He never did, as he quickly fell asleep over a long book but my mother read it. She believed every word of it and could not conceive how a man could sit down and invent the story of Squire Allworthy and Sophia and Tom out of his head. So did Robert Owen before her read *Robinson Crusoe* and Richardson's novels and believe every word to be true. But my mother was fifty before she read a novel and to her dying day she had not completely grasped the nature of fiction or of drama. The then current attitude is well shown by this sentence from a contemporary lecture by a leading Welsh preacher and Doctor of Divinity :

" Novels, the disgrace of English literature, and the curse of multitudes of English readers, do not take with Welsh readers."


## II

The Upper and Lower Rhymney Schools were transformed from British to Board Schools on the passing of the Education Act of 1870 and the like change befell the National or Middle Rhymney School provided by the Iron Company in 1858. The nonconformist ministers were in the forefront of the demand for the change. They had been the managers and examiners of the British Schools and were probably glad to be rid of the financial anxiety attached to them. Government grants were made partly on the basis of attendances and partly on the basis of examination results. Funds were raised by lectures and entertainments and by school fees, but these were often in arrears, especially during strikes and lock-outs and the frequent epidemics of small-pox, scarlet fever, and measles. In the lower standards fees were a penny a week and in the higher twopence. Married women teachers continued to be employed until 1909.

George Berry Kovachich, certificated in the third division of the third degree, and his wife Emma, certificated in the second division of the first degree, had taken up their respective posts of master and mistress in the Upper Rhymney School in August, 1868, and they entered on their duties with all the efficiency of new brooms. The school was closed for a fortnight for cleaning. Bell, ink, pens and paper, chairs and slates, black boards and easels, registers and sewing materials were ordered and windows were mended. They found ink supplied in a troublesome way, in small stone bottles resting on the desks and removed at the close of each lesson. They ordered ink-wells. The ink itself came in casks from Abergavenny. They started a night school with 34 present and this number quickly rose to over a hundred. It was the era of monitors and pupil teachers. The pupil teachers were instructed by the master at 8 or 8-30 a.m. and also in the night school. They caused as much trouble as the children, if not more. They were often late, or supine, or obtuse. They forgot their maps or showed an unaccountable reluctance to attend to grammar or recited poetry without any indication that they understood it. One had to be fetched in from playing marbles after school had begun; another was caught reading a newspaper behind a blackboard when he should have been engaged with his class.

"Had an unpleasant affair with the senior male teacher. He pushed a girl out of the classroom so violently that she fell headlong. Upon remonstrating, perhaps rather strongly, he replied in insubordinate language and manner, upon which I had to chastise him or else good-bye to authority."

So runs a passage in the record which the conscientious master kept faithfully day by day from August 31st, 1868, until February 2nd, 1877, within a week of his sudden death. The entries, brief though they are, throw a light on the problems of the school and on the conditions of the village.

Committees and tradesmen, then as since, were dilatory :

8-12-69. " Mr. Jones changing stoves at last, the Committee driven to this not from love to the school but from fear of losing a Club that holds its meetings in the upper schoolroom."

" Storms throughout the week unceasing. Slates flying off the roof. Months since wrote to the Committee. Providential that the falling slates have not yet caused the death of some child or other."

5-4-70. " Mrs. Kovachich waited upon Mr. John Lewis (a manager) anent a dusting brush and duster. After nearly an hour's intercession obtained two sevenpenny brushes for school use."

School routine was frequently interrupted by some local custom or event.

2-1-71. " Opened school at the usual time but with less than two dozen children it being *le jour de l'an*, the children about the streets besieging every one for a New Year's gift, many of the shopkeepers close their establishments, appearing to dread the interruption as the Easterns do the ravages of the Armies of the Lord. Waited an hour and then dismissed."

6-1-73. " Influx of work boys who only purpose remaining as long as the strike continues or they are driven to work elsewhere. Most of them are as wild as the ' untaught Indian's brood '.

28-1-73. " School noisy. The uncouth savages from the mines do not appear to known the simplest forms of decency. Kept the whole afternoon school in in the afternoon in a state of silence as a matter of discipline. Teachers very supine."

25-3-73. " Influx of work boys has ceased and those who came to school some three months since have taken their departure as prospect of long protracted strike coming to an end this week."

24-9-74. " Harvest Thanksgiving in the Church, District Meeting of the Welsh Wesleyans, Penywaun Pig and Cattle Fair, together with a public demonstration of the Foresters prevented children assembling in the afternoon, therefore dismissed the few who came, no school, registers not marked."

Other interruptions recorded are tea parties and eisteddfods ; colliery explosions, funerals, and the Cymro-Hibernian riots ; the school was wanted as a polling booth ; it broke up at twelve for the man to whitewash ; Gwilym Hiraethog was preaching at Zion Chapel. On the days following these disturbances " a little lassitude is apparent in scholars and teachers." " No lesson learnt—too full of the Circus for that." Weather was an important factor. In summer children were kept away because they were busy carrying water from the wells ; in winter by rain, snow and frost. On January 8th, 1869, we read : " This completes the seventh week in which it has rained every day more or less, generally more." An entry a few days later is not surprising : " School work not up to the mark, probably the deficiency is as much in myself as in the school as I am suffering from sore throat and severe cold." And again : " Must have recourse to patience and chalk."

But this is recorded not remembered history. I remember very little of these years in the Upper School. There was a teacher with a sweet face and flaxen hair whom I loved ; there was a day when I was about to be punished for some misdeed by the large and formidable headmaster when the small and brisk Mrs. Kovachich (Govash for short) pleaded successfully for mercy ; there was the chanting in unison of the geography lessons and multiplication table, as prescribed by Pestalozzi :

Northumberland—Newcastle—on the Tyne
Durham—Durham—on the Wear
Yorkshire—York—on the Ouse

right through the fifty-two counties, followed by a musical tour round the capes, finishing with a crescendo at

North Foreland and South Foreland in KENT.

I remember nothing more about lessons until I came under Daniel Thomas, the successor to Mr. Kovachich. We called him Mishtir Bach because of the contrast in their bulk, and they differed in other ways. Mr. Kovachich had been a local preacher with the Wesleyans ; the hobby of Daniel Thomas was politics. He vanished daily at the morning break, to a neighbouring bakehouse, where in a cloud of smoke he discussed with a group of Liberal shopkeepers the morning news— the exploits of Mr. Gladstone, the iniquities of Disraeli, Disestablishment, and the Sunday Closing Act. One of the group was the local Liberal agent and it fell to him to inform Mr. Gladstone that Rhymney Liberals would give him " every legitimate support and assistance in its power " and it was a red-letter morning in the bakehouse when T. N. Evans read to the gathering :

I am directed by Mr. Gladstone to inform you that he has received the communication which you have done him the honour to send him and to convey to you his thanks for the expression of approval and confidence in Her Majesty's Government which it contains.

On such occasions Mishtir Bach was apt to refill his pipe and exceed the quarter of an hour allowed in the time table at eleven o'clock for recreation.

Daniel Thomas was for many years a director of the Rechabite Society and it was he who translated into Welsh the Ritual and Rules of the Order. He was more musical than his predecessor, and taught us solfa from a Modulator. We had to sing three songs to the inspectors on examination day : the *Emigrant Ship*, the *Bells*, and the *Canadian Boat Song* and in due course they reported in their characteristic style : " The singing is of a good class and well chosen." The school managers were frequent visitors. Once when the master was away ill two ministers arrived to help the assistant mistress to keep order and we sang appropriately the *Old Black Cat* and *Don't Fret*. But the song which made the deepest impression on me went something like this :

> Neath the white waves they have laid him
> Far, far away from the shore,
> Where the coral rocks are shading,
> And the sea birds flutter o'er
> The poor little sailor boy,
> The poor little sailor boy.

Our memories were exercised and our vocabularies enriched by learning hundreds of lines from Scott and Byron. I have forgotten all but four but they have been useful. When no one has known what to say when watching a sunset I have quoted with effect :

The western waves of ebbing day
Rolled o'er the glen their level way,
Each purple peak, each flinty spire
Was bathed in floods of living fire.

No one who was present can forget the examination day ; it was like a funeral and the Judgement Day rolled into one. The hectic preparation at home, the girls in their spotless pina-fores, the boys doubly brushed and scrubbed ; the arrival of that terrifying ogre, Her Majesty's Inspector, with his strange English name, the agony of trying to get the two halves of the freehand drawing to balance each other with the frantic aid of india-rubber. And this is how the headmaster recorded the event :

May 25. Day of Examination of H.M.I. and his assistants. Many of the children assembled shortly after 8 a.m. Mr. Waddington kept the infants waiting for him until after one o'clock and consequently they were tired and restless. A very wet day and hence some absenteeism amounting to £6 8s.

But there were other and happier days when we passed notes surreptitiously under the desks to the girls, making amorous appointments to meet them at the back of the romantic coal yard, half afraid, in the dusk, and this clandestine correspondence led to many jealousies, quarrels and reconciliations. Between the coalyard and the High Street gardens we rummaged among the rubbish heaps for corks which when found we took to Mrs. Wiltshire's and bartered at the rate of six corks for a bottle of pop.

I recall that on a back bench there sat some quite grown-up young men who had returned to school from the pits to prepare themselves for one of the theological colleges on their way to becoming ministers of the gospel. This was before the establishment of the intermediate schools.

" In the first place God made idiots. This was for practice. Then he made school boards." So a well-known educator has written and there were persons in Rhymney who agreed with him. Controversy was always raging around the actions of the new Board. The Upper School was overcrowded and at one stage 120 boys of the higher standards were ordered to transfer themselves to the Middle Rhymney School. But the master there was a Tory and the school was tainted with its old National associations. The parents insisted on their right to choose. Public meetings to protest against the change were speedily summoned and within six weeks the order was rescinded. Two years later the attempt was renewed and the Board threatened to turn the school into one for girls only. Again the Board was defeated and the problem was then solved by re-building.

Religious instruction in the schools was for years the subject of violent controversy and elections were fought upon it. In our eyes the reactionary State Church blocked the road to civil liberty. The 25th Section of the Education Act of 1870 entitled School Boards to pay the school pence of the children of indigent parents at whatever school, denominational or otherwise, selected by the parents. This involved a cardinal principle. " It is a small matter," said the parson. " So " replied John Morley, barrister-at-law, in a contemporary pamphlet, " was the yeoman's house at Hougomont and so were Hampden's twenty shillings." Usually the Church candidates headed the list because of the concentration of their supporters upon them, whereas the nonconformist vote was scattered among numerous sects, who would not agree to eliminate the candidates of any. It was March, 1883, before the practice of reading the Bible was permitted by the Board. It was then read from 9 to 9-30 a.m.

There is an illuminating report of a meeting of the Bedwellty School Board in the *Western Mail* for 10th May, 1877, shewing how at that time leading Welsh nonconformist ministers regarded Rhymney as belonging to England rather than Wales. It is worth quoting in full :

Correspondence was read having reference to the grant from Government to be applied towards the University College of Wales.

Rev. E. Davies :—I don't see that we have anything to do with this, as we do not live in Wales. We are not classified with Welsh School Boards. The Blue Book puts us in Monmouthshire, outside of Wales. Oxford is nearer to us a good deal than Aberystwyth.

Rev. R. Williams :—I agree with you.

Rev. E. Davies :—We have no business with it, and I move that it be laid on the table.

No demur was made to the proposal, which was accordingly adopted.

No mention of Welsh as a class subject is made before 1895, when it was being taught " with praiseworthy success in the two lowest standards and in the fourth." " Hen Wlad fy Nhadau ", the national anthem, now appears among the songs learnt and among the recitations are *Llongau Madog, Yr Afonig,* and *Y Wennol Gyntaf.* In 1868 Mr. Kovachich had entered in his diary :

Find the Welsh language a hindrance to their progress in English as it is Welsh in the home, in society, and in the chapel.

No Welsh was spoken or taught in school in my time and this fact tended to oust it from the home and the street. I have been told that we spoke Welsh at home until I was about six and that thereafter as the children went to school the family turned to English and reserved Welsh for the purposes of religion. We learnt the scriptures and hymns in Welsh and listened weekly to Welsh sermons. I never had any lesson in the grammar of the language either at school or college and have always been handicapped when attempting to write idiomatic Welsh for publication and more than once had recourse to expert help.

My Somerset grandmother, Harriet Cook, learnt to speak and read Welsh and so did my mother. At that time, as to this day, more Welsh was spoken in the upper part of the town where they lived than in middle Rhymney where we lived.

When discussing bilingualism in *My Life and Thought*, Albert Schweitzer tells us that it is only self-deception if any one believes that he has two mother tongues. "He may think he is equally master of each yet it is invariably the case that he habitually thinks only in one, and is only in that one free and creative." That has been my experience. The restriction of Welsh to the offices of religion, residence out of Wales for the greater part of one's life, the absence of the practice in daily speech of a living dialect has meant that such Welsh as I possess is bookish and not that of the home and the market place.

III

Out of school we played games, some in the High Street and some at the back of our house between it and the coalyard where a stream thickened with coal dust ran near some pig styes. We dammed its muddy waters into a pond and then suddenly opened the sluices and flooded the land, dooming our paper boats to instant destruction. We did this a thousand times and went home wild with joy, wet, dirty, excited, and as proud as the builders of the dams on the Nile.

The games that children play are similar in all ages and in all countries. The harmless art of knucklebones, wrote Stevenson, has seen the fall of the Roman Empire and the rise of the United States. I do not suppose that Rhymney has changed in this respect in fifty years, except that the motorists have driven from the streets such children as they have not maimed or killed. Even in our far off days we had to get out of the way of Bill Edwards mounted on his penny-farthing bicycle showing off up and down High Street.

We bowled iron hoops on the pavement, spun tops, stalked on stilts, stuck leather suckers on window panes, blew soap-bubbles out of saucers, by means of a clay pipe, played marbles, leap frog, I spy. At the back of the house we played rounders and cricket and a game akin to them called " bat and catty." We flew kites and banged bladders about which we got from the slaughter house of the Company Shop. Girls skipped and hopped on the pavement and played duckstones much as I saw girls play in the streets of Marakesch the other day.

There was an active trade in marbles. We carried our bags like oriental merchants in a bazaar. I was in a privileged position because whenever my father went to Bristol on business he brought me back a rich assortment of alley taws, glass and blood alleys, bowlers and bompers with which I could drive hard bargains in exchange for the commoner sort.

We played a bouncing rubber ball against the pine-end of a house, or we placed our caps on the ground in a row against the wall and pitched a ball into them from a distance of seven or eight feet. The boy in whose hat the ball rested had to pick it up and hit one of the others with it while they scampered away.

We played pranks, threading door knockers with black cotton and hiding in dark passages until scared away by the police or an irate housekeeper. There were tunnels to give spice to adventure, one under the surgery and Lawn, and one between the cemetery and the Barracks Road. Or we went further afield near the isolated powder house, to a disused and forsaken pit-shaft into which we dropped stones and listened spell-bound to the resounding thuds as the stones struck the sides, fell into the booming waters, and sank into eternity.

We watched the grown ups make " the pond'rous quoit obliquely fall ", or followed them with ferrets in their pockets and dogs at their heels when they went ratting around the pig styes. There were frequent cricket matches and a legend was handed down that one of the batsmen, Bill Lewis, a Falstaffian figure though a mere clerk, had hit a ball from the cricket field near the vicarage through a bedroom window in the house of the colliery manager at the Terrace—an incredible distance.

We had pancakes on Ash Wednesday and ducked for apples in the wooden wash-tub at Halloween. On wet days we dabbled with paint boxes and crayons which were more satisfying than freehand drawing, or we put gaily coloured pictures and transfers into scrap books, or played with photographs and a stereoscope. In the home of the Trumps there was a toy theatre made out of a tea chest with a Christmas almanac for drop curtain. I helped to slide the cardboard characters on and off and read aloud my part in the *Miller and his Men* which had the burning of the mill for grand climax. The Trump family hailed from Honiton in Devon and the grandfather of the boys with whom I played was "qualified to practise the Veterinary Art" as testified by a certificate signed by John Abernethy and Astley Cooper on the 9th May, 1825. He came to Rhymney to take charge of the Company's horses and stables, and his son Henry Valentine became in due course General Manager and enjoyed the unique distinction in our community of being able to speak French.

For us children there were also annual excitements in the shape of Sanger's Circus, Wombwell's Menagerie, Poole's Myriorama, and Studt's Coach and Horses. For some strange reason of chapel ethics I was forbidden the circus but allowed to visit the wild beasts. It was explained that the animals were the creatures of God and I was left to infer that red nosed clowns and acrobats in tights were limbs of Satan. My perplexity was not lessened when I was taken by my father to the circus entrance to collect, on behalf of the Company, the rent for the pitch from the enormously fat wife of the proprietor. They were always fat and there was always a litter of agile children. The sight around the circus at night time was thrilling, the side shows lit with yellow naptha flares, the shouting showmen, the noisy merry-go-rounds, the shooting galleries, the boxing saloons (with a flaming tinman called Bill Samuel offering to fight anybody for five pounds a side), the billy-fair play which provided a little mild gambling and rewarded the winner with a clock or a china dog for the penny risked. And of course, there were quacks with infallible remedies.

> See here comes a fine carriage, how gaily it goes,
> With a big burly black and a ring in his nose,
> He has lotion and potion and pills that are rare
> To cure all the sick ones that come on the Square.

During the night they folded their tents, like the Arabs, and disappeared with the dawn to Dowlais or Tredegar, leaving a ring of sawdust on the ground, where the piebald horses had proudly circled to the crack of the whip.

It was in Rhymney that John Studt gave his first performance of *Sea on Land*, substituting rocking boats for rocking horses. The change was so successful that he now reposes under the most conspicuous tombstone in Cardiff cemetery.

Near the Castle Hotel periodically appeared Noakes' Theatre, a wooden structure, which I was not allowed to enter on religious grounds, but I sometimes peeped through the joints and got a glimpse of the stage. Among the plays whose names I recall from the handbills were the *Maid of Cefn Ydfa*, the *Murder at the Red Barn, Silver King, East Lynne* and *Maria Martin*. I must have been over thirteen before I entered a theatre, for the first play I saw was not published until 1883. I saw it in Merthyr. It was *Called Back* by Hugh Conway, a Bristol auctioneer, and it had a big circulation as a book. All I remember of it is the procession of a convoy of prisoners chained together marching across the stage through ice and snow on their way to Siberia in the cruel days of Czardom.

Other visitors to Rhymney were the Breton boys hawking strings of dried onions; Italians who came to sell plaster statuettes which they balanced on a board on their heads; stocking sellers from West Wales carrying a supply suspended from a yoke on the shoulders; Scottish packmen who peddled drapery; and German Bands, three or four sad and miserable wandering performers in blue uniforms from across the Rhine, who played through the streets, often in the rain, for a few coppers.

We had no orchestras of our own, but we produced music from a variety of instruments; a tooth comb and paper, clappers made of bone (castanets), a tin whistle, a flute, a concertina, an accordion. We also extracted a noise from a Jew's harp, called by us aligiwga, if that is the way to write it. Giwga is English *gewgaw* and is current only in parts of South Wales. In the Swansea valley the form is *biwba*, the labials taking the place of gutterals. The pundits find *ali* more difficult to explain. *Ali* is used in Welsh for a marble and for the glass stopper on a bottle of " pop ". Another suggestion is that it is a corruption of English *hurly*, meaning tumult, uproar. The strangest things happen in dialect borrowings from a foreign language and it is not impossible that *hurly* should be transmogrified into *ali*.

No chapel had then an organ. They had doleful, wheezy harmoniums. There were a few pianos in the houses of the better-off and in some villages public classes were held on Saturdays for teaching pupils to play the new instrument. Years later at the " opening " of the organ in Ebenezer Chapel the organist sat down to play the voluntary to the expectant congregation but no sound came forth. On going round to the blower, Will Jones, Ffair Rhos, Will retorted that he could not blow without a music book.

# CHAPTER IV

## EARLIEST MEMORIES

*There is nothing, Sir, too little for so little a creature as man.*
                                                              DR. JOHNSON.

*One needs only to be old enough to be as young as one will.*
                                                              HENRY ADAMS.

I HAVE known a man who has given convincing proof that he remembers the toys placed in his stocking at his second Christmas. I can claim no such powers. I have, for example, lived in many houses for a year or longer, fifteen to twenty of them, and now find it difficult to distinguish the features of one from the other with precision. I do remember that the front door and window frames of 100, High Street had the distinction of being grained a golden brown with a comb and then varnished, a sure sign of respectability. At its centre the door had a large knob of cut glass of many small shining facets. I can put no date to my first experience of scents and sounds ; the hawthorn on the Barracks Road, the lilac tree at the end of the red gravel path of our garden, the cawing of the rooks in the Lawn, the tolling of the bells calling the faithful to church on Sunday mornings and evenings, and the engines coughing black smoke. The lilac tree is mixed up in my later memory with Whitman's poem on the death of Lincoln which opens, " When lilacs last in the door yard bloom'd."

I was five when I saw men near the churchyard breaking stones for road metal to qualify for relief during the lock-out of 1875. The manager of the Works, Richard Laybourne, in his capacity of chairman of the Local Board had supplied the stone, moved by the deep distress, and when he reported the purchase he added that the distress was too great to be grappled with by breaking six hundred tons of limestone. So I was to learn years later. It was during this lock-out that the workless and starving men forced their way into the Lawn and on to the steps of the Manager's house, demanding to see him. He professed to be suffering from a cold and unable to come outside, but he agreed to receive a deputation of three. When they returned the leader reported as follows : " The manager says that times are very bad and there is little or no work and it is impossible to pay the wages demanded. His advice is that the Englishmen should go back to England, the Scotch to Scotland, the Irish to Ireland." A voice from the crowd : " Where are the Welsh to go ? " " They can go to hell ! "

I remember seeing on the way to Rhymney Bridge a loco-motive engine tumbled on its side on the sloping bank between the railway and the river and great wooden beams, still there, thrown across the river in order to get the engine away. I remember being told to go to chapel on a week night and going instead to a room at the back of the Castle Hotel to see a con-jurer, who took a watch, put it in a small bag, smashed it to pieces with a hammer and then took it out whole. Coming away we were chased by a dog. I caught my foot in the first rail of a tramroad and my forehead struck the second rail. There was a gash which the doctor sewed up with five stitches and to this day I bear about me the marks of my first remembered disobedience and my fall, in a faint scar on my brow. I remember a picture in the *Penny Illustrated London News* of the death of the Prince Imperial from the assegais of the Zulus, drawn, I suppose, by Caton Woodville. But this must have been in 1879. Pictures of this sort were on view in the window of the local stationer's on Friday and Saturdays nights and could be seen for nothing.

Three generations of the Redwood family have served our community faithfully as doctors, and during that period there have been great changes in the vital statistics. For example :

| Year. | Birth-rate. | Death-rate. |
|---|---|---|
| 1882 | 33.56 | 26.73 |
| 1892 | 36.80 | 18.72 |
| 1902 | 40.08 | 21.55 |
| 1912 | 30.01 | 14.09 |
| 1922 | 25.66 | 13.66 |
| 1932 | 18.3 | 13.3 |
| England and Wales | 15.3 | 12.0 |

Year after year the Dr. Redwood of the day reported on the shocking housing conditions in certain areas, but little or nothing was done before the turn of the century. From 1882 to 1900 inclusive, only 51 new houses were erected ; then with a change in the composition of the District Council and in the attitude of the Central Government, 969 houses were built between 1901 and 1919 inclusive.

A sewerage scheme was adopted in 1896 and an agreement for a Joint Sewerage Board for the Rhymney Valley was signed in 1910 and became effective in 1912. The Cottage Hospital was built by the workmen in 1902-1903. But these developments fall outside my period, as do a number of other institutions such as the Drill Hall (1910), the Cinema (1913), the Public Park (1920), the Bowling Green and Tennis Court (1925). The arrival of these later amenities coincided with the closing of the coalpits : New Dyffryn (1921), Mardy (1925), Tynewydd (1927). The War Memorial was unveiled in October, 1929, with 120 names on the Roll of Honour.

Typhoid, scarlet fever, measles and phthisis, croup and whooping cough were endemic. Men and women threw fits ; warts, ringworm and mumps were common afflictions. Among disagreeable medicines of childhood I recall Norway tar, senna and wormwood. Superstitious and surreptitious remedies abounded. My mother sent for the midwife to cure my warts and she did so by telling me to spit on them when waking in the morning. Meanwhile she would bury a piece of fat bacon in the garden and in nine days they would disappear. They did. In 1935 I met Mr. A. F. Luttrell at his house at East Quantoxhead near Dunster Castle. He said that locally warts were reputed to be cured by smearing the slime of snails on them. He also told me this story. A local farmer had sixty sheep which died. He sent for a white witch. She came and stuck pins into a sheep's heart and hung it up in the fireplace to keep danger from descending through the chimney. No more sheep died.

Some years ago in Rhymney a doctor was summoned to one of the small cottages where a child was ill with pneumonia. The stench about the bed was such that he threw back the clothes and found the lungs of a sheep against the feet of the child, placed there, the grandmother explained, to draw into them the poison from the child's lungs. Cow dung was used as a poultice for boils and carbuncles, and the water in which the blacksmith had cooled his red-hot irons was drunk as an

iron tonic to strengthen the blood. Warm urine was believed
to be a cure for a fresh wound, and the juice of the house leek
for earache. Whole pages of local newspapers were filled
for years with standing advertisements of balms and balsams,
pills and powders. Copies passed mysteriously from hand
to hand of an illustrated pocket edition of Aristotle's *Complete
Master Piece* " displaying the Secrets of Nature in the Generation
of Man." We told fortunes from tea leaves, threw spilt salt
across the left shoulder, dreaded crossed knives. Servant
girls kept a Book of Dreams hidden under their pillows and
puzzled over their destiny in secret.

We had in our midst a family who furnished not only
Rhymney but South Wales with generations of bone-setters.
This is their story as given to me.

Thomas Jones was born in Cardiganshire in 1800, and
he was brought up in a farm at Penalltgoch in South Cardiganshire, not far from Manordeifi. He was particularly skilful
in the treatment of injuries and diseases of animals and his
services were much in demand in Cardiganshire. He came
to Rhymney to visit his son, and at that time there was a disease
prevalent amongst pigs on the Rhymney Iron Co.'s. farms
which they had found intractable. Thomas Jones was called
in to see them and as a result of the treatment he prescribed
the disease was stamped out. He died and was buried at Rhymney
in 1855.

His son, Thomas Rocyn Jones, who was born at Penalltgoch, came to live at Rhymney and was for some years
employed at the Iron Works. He also was skilful in the treatment of animals, but extended his practice to the treatment
of human injuries and acquired a considerable reputation as
a bone-setter in South Wales and the border counties. He was

particularly skilful in the treatment of fractures, dislocations and various injuries of muscles and joints. He was also conversant with the orthodox surgical treatment of these injuries, apart from his own original method of treatment, for he had a good library on the orthodox treatment of injuries. He undoubtedly saved many limbs from amputation and restored cripple joints to full function. He had devised wooden splints with a foot-piece, which were quite unknown to the profession, and he was fond of moulding gutta-percha splints for keeping the hand in dorsiflexion in cases of paralysis and severe injuries of tendons. He had also invented a resinous plaster spread on linen which was formed into bandages and when applied was an effective splint for sprains and lesser injuries of joints. Another device was the application of leather wedges to inner sides of the soles of shoes in the case of flat foot. The dorsiflexion splints and the wedges are mentioned because they belonged to his common practice at least 50 years before they became accepted in the profession.

A story is told of him that when walking from Dowlais Top to Rhymney during one dark night he was waylaid by two men, but whom he fortunately was able to master. The next day one of these men turned up at Thomas Rocyn Jones' surgery at Rhymney Bridge with an injured shoulder. He recognised the assailant of the previous evening, and to the latter's astonishment he was reminded of the episode. The shoulder, however, was treated, but perhaps with a little more vigour on this occasion than was actually necessary, but none the less the assailant left the surgery very grateful for the benefit he had received.

There are all sorts of legends about him all over South Wales, and even to this day one meets very old people who were treated by him. His services were held in great esteem and a portrait in oils of himself was presented to him. When he died, in 1877, at the age of 55—the same age as his father—the public erected a monument over his grave.

When he died his son, Thomas Rocyn Jones, carried on his practice, but he died within a few years.

The practice then passed to the elder son, David Rocyn Jones who was born at Rhymney in 1847, and died in 1915. He achieved as great a reputation as his father, and as far as one can judge was as skilful a bone-setter as his father and grandfather before him. From my own personal observation of him I can testify that he was extraordinarily dexterous as a manipulator, with a sure instinct for the right type of case that was likely to benefit by manipulation. He had powerful arms and wrists, and was very quick both in his movements and in his thinking. In addition he was no mean musician, had a good tenor voice, and was secretary and choirmaster at Moriah chapel. His services for many years were in great request as a bone-setter, and he was frequently called professionally over the Border to the English counties of Gloucester, Wiltshire and Shropshire.

The fifth generation of this Rhymney family is today represented by the Medical Officer of Health for Monmouthshire and by an orthopaedic surgeon in Harley Street each of whom has added a professional training to his native inheritance ; it is also represented by a third brother who continues in South Wales the practice in the traditional way of what today is called manipulative surgery.

I remember going many times between eight and nine at night with another small boy to take his father's supper to the steel mill, where the father was a tall and thirsty roller-man. We swelled with importance moving bravely through the dark, among the ghostly shadows, picking our way past the Bessemer plant over the rail bank, until we reached the mill where we watched the white hot ingots being wheeled along on iron carriages with long handles, tipped down first to the roughers and then to the rollers, and squeezed out into longer and longer, thinner and thinner, straighter and straighter strips of steel rails, shaped and cut to the right length, then cooled and piled up on the bank, and presently sent to Cardiff or Newport to be shipped to the ends of the world. There still lies prone among the ruins of the Works, or there did until quite recently, a single rail eighty feet long which was rolled for some Exhibition. For many years it was preserved in a long office corridor and shown with pride to visitors as the longest rail in the world.

It was in June, 1881, that electric light was introduced to Rhymney. Many hundreds of people gathered to see the rail bank lit up at night for the first time by means of the Brush system.

I can date exactly one vivid memory and like many such it is associated with death. Bernard Shaw once told me that his earliest memory was of a body of a drowned man laid out on the quays in Dublin under a tarpaulin but with hands uncovered and they were very white. Mrs. Shaw's first recollection was of a placard announcing the assassination of Abraham Lincoln. I was eight years old. I was taken to Ebbw Vale to an uncle's funeral and saw his coffin emerge with difficulty from a bedroom window and slide down a plank on to the shoulders of the bearers, it being too big to be brought down by the narrow staircase of the tiny cottage.

No child in the Rhymney of that time can forget the silent procession of miners through the street after a colliery explosion when those hurt or killed were carried home on stretchers and then the anxiety as to which house in the row was destined to receive the still living or the dead father or son.

But most of all do I remember funerals and their accompaniments. Death in a mining community is a familiar but not commonplace occurrence. It brought so much suffering in its train that all minds were concerned and all hearts affected. " It may be my turn next " was the pitman's inevitable reflection. A new born baby might be christened on its father's coffin. When I went away to college the staple news in my mother's weekly letters was the illness, or misfortune or death of a neighbour ; births were rarely mentioned, marriages never. Neighbourhood with us covered most of the population of eight thousand, for I knew somebody in nearly every family through the chapels, the choirs, the Shop or the Works.

There was an elaborate funeral ritual calculated to deepen the impression of death. Clothes played a large and expensive part in the ceremony, and were a frequent origin of debt. There were three drapers then in Rhymney, James Griffiths at the top of the village, John Griffiths in the middle, and Thomas Griffiths at the lower end, their establishments known respectively as Albion, Commerce, and Cuba. What the island of Cuba had to do with drapery I never found out. Although ourselves dependent on the Company Shop we sometimes extended our orders for mourning to one or other of the three, and especially the last as he was a deacon in Brynhyfryd. We were usually in mourning for some one in the wide Welsh circle of our relatives and twice death entered our own household and took young children away. It was the period of smooth black cloth with a satin sheen, crape, velvet and jet, black bordered handkerchiefs and notepaper and mourning cards, hat bands and streamers. For the better-off, graves would be bricked and coffins would be of polished mahogany and brass studs, for the poorer folk coffins would be of common wood covered with black cloth and black studs. A prayer meeting was held at the home of the dead on the eve of the burial. Relatives would come from far and near, all the way from Cardiganshire, for example, to attend the funeral. Food would be prepared for them. There was always a buxom, buoyant and managing aunt who took charge and pressed the cold boiled ham on the visitors. The neighbours gathered. There was a trickle of whispered conversation, about the weather, the last funeral, the next funeral, the absent son in America, or the wayward daughter in the big city. The minister, supported by the deacons, read and prayed. The incomparable hymn and tune followed—any one of half a dozen could pitch the tune and the undertaker could also do so as part of his professional equipment. Questions of precedence in the procession among the relatives would have been settled after much heart burning. The Oddfellows or the Buffaloes in full regalia would be drawn up outside ready to lead the way with staves and ribbons. The nonconformist cemetery on the hillside was a mile away and was reached at the end of a steep and stony path which made those immediately behind the coffin tremble for its safety. The coffin was lowered by the male next-of-kin. I still see the gravedigger in corduroy trousers and boots stiff with clay, the only person not in black, leaning on his spade among the tombstones, which, like the coffins below, betrayed our indigenous snobbery and carried our hatred of equality into the presence of the great Leveller. The drawn blinds, the unusual clothes, the unnatural silence, the ticking of the grand-father's clock, and all that followed from home to graveyard and back again stamped itself indelibly on a child's mind.

Now and then I found myself at a " Church " funeral. Here the attraction was the reading of the Burial Service by the vicar, Canon Evans, whose popularity can be measured by the fact that he shared with Andrew Buchan the honour of having his large round benevolent countenance stamped on jugs and mugs sold at the Company Shop. He intoned the service in a melodious and consoling voice, which rose imperceptibly into the Welsh *hwyl*, bearing the congregation aloft far above and beyond the open grave. When he himself, who had buried so many, came to die he left four requests : that his coffin should be of elm ; that no hearse should be employed ; that no bricks should be used in the grave ; and that no flowers should be sent.

Babies arrived with disturbing frequency in our home and so greatly displeased the eldest son at some point in the series that he felt as Tess did when she grew older, quite a Malthusian towards his mother for thoughtlessly giving him so many little sisters and brothers. On these occasions, besides the midwife, there would be always around a kind and competent cousin, Ann White Row, a miner's wife who tip-toed up and downstairs on mysterious errands.

Rooms are associated with events; for example, a bedroom in which I was stripped and thrashed for helping myself to biscuits from a barrel in the Company Shop, at a time when I was too young to know that the shop did not belong to us. Our furniture was of the period : red or yellow mahogany bedroom suites, black horse-hair chairs and sofas, dark malachite clocks, a grandfather's clock its face figured with the phases of the moon, Nottingham lace curtains, beaded footstools, spittoons, family albums. Strips of drugget protected the best carpet. Screens made of ribbons of coloured paper kept the wind from blowing through the bedroom grates. In bed we wore night caps. There was no bathroom in 100, High Street; we were washed " all over " on Friday nights in a tub in front of the kitchen fire. Later when we moved to the Terrace we had a bathroom, and we had Venetian blinds in the parlour. The recurring babies wore quilted bibs and were rocked in a wooden cradle, painted red. We had gas in both houses but kept unused a handsome ornamental porcelain lamp in the parlour where there was also a large gilt mirror over the mantelpiece. Oil lamps were used in the smaller houses and paraffin was hawked through the streets to the sound of a bell. The price of gas remained stationary for many years at 4s. 6d. per 1,000 cubic feet. On our sideboard stood a painted ship, upon a painted ocean of green paper within a glass shade. You pulled a string which revolved a metal cylinder bristling with minute teeth. The waves rose and fell charmed by a tinkling melody, the work perhaps of Mozart himself. We know that at his latter end the Master wrote for such musical toys, driven by grim necessity. Close by was a walnut writing box filled with pens, pencils, penknives, and pocket books which my father brought back from his periodic visits to Bristol.

For pictures we had German prints of Ruth and Boaz, Red Riding Hood, and a highly etherealized portrait of William Williams, Pantycelyn, looking the angelic hymn-writer he was. One day this picture fell on the parlour floor and my mother foretold " bad news " and sure enough next morning we heard of the death of a distant relative. At Christmas grocers gave away oleographic calendars. On our kitchen mantelpiece stood a row of brass candlesticks, symmetrically graded in size, with gophering irons at the ends for frilling flounces, and a tea canister in the centre.

The fire-irons, fender, stand, and toasting fork were of burnished steel probably made, *sub rosa*, by some craftsman in the Works. On other mantelpieces stood white and gold china spaniels. Sets of ancestral china in corner cupboards and rows of lustre jugs on dressers were a much cherished possession of the colliers' wives. We had no " settle " at right angles to the fireplace but there was one in Penuel Row, where also there was a baking oven. Sometimes we had our bread baked there ; at other times I used to take the dough in a tin balanced on my head to be baked in Sun Row at a penny a loaf. For a summer drink we had small beer made of herbs for which I made a weekly journey to the brewery for a pennorth of barm to make it rise.

" The housewife's store of linen, or the man's store of books or the tools of his trade were the best examples of a habit of mind which, in weaker moments, led to accumulating trinkets, souvenirs, and half-broken bric-a-brac, and covering the walls with vastly enlarged photographs of several generations of the family." This sentence written by the late Mendelssohn Bartholdy to describe the average German attitude to household possessions before the War is exactly applicable to the wife of the collier and craftsman in the Rhymney of my youth. " To their owners all these things were much more in the nature of living pets than objects of marketable value to be bought or sold." For young women it was the age of the bottom drawer, and for young men of the English lever watch and silver chain across the waistcoat. Which reminds me that we had one watchmaker in our High Street who advertised " English levers at Coventry prices " in the local press. He had a thick Colonel Blimp moustache which drooped heavily over his mouth and down the sides. We liked to peep at him with a magnifying glass stuck on his eye picking up minute screws and springs. When a customer entered he still held the glass fixed. He was always in arrears with repairs but it mattered little because he was always willing to trust a customer with the loan of a watch.

One memory provokes another. I have seen more monocles in our Foreign Office in an afternoon than in Rhymney in twenty years. In fact I recall only one, worn by a barrister turned solicitor and then coroner. He was also distinguished in our community by wearing a silk top-hat weekdays and Sundays and not only at funerals. Once when addressing a Baptist Assembly on the Marriage Act he said : " The law of the Lord is perfect making wise the simple ; but the laws of man are full of holes and in those holes the lawyers live."

One other costume attracted and puzzled us during the school holidays. It was that of a hatless blue-coat boy, wearing white bands, silver buttons, belt, yellow stockings, and buckled shoes. He was to become " a Welsh International " and a Canon of the Church.

# CHAPTER V

## MORE SCHOOLING

*Useless to tell him (the barbarian, the Philistine) that these
are the keys that unlock the gates of Paradise unless somehow
you can give him a taste for Paradise. And how can you give him
that? Only, I suppose, by giving him a glimpse of Paradise.
And how a glimpse is to be given I am sure I do not know; but
I can see it is what education ought to do.*

CLIVE BELL (*Civilisation*).

WHEN I was between eleven and twelve I was put to try
for a scholarship at Pengam School, seven miles down
the valley. This was a school founded and endowed by Edward
Lewis, a member of the Van family of Caerphilly, from the
senior branch of which the Earls of Plymouth are descended
through the female line. Edward Lewis died unmarried in
1728 at the early age of 37. In his early twenties, in 1715,
he made a will which included bequests for the poor of Gelligaer,
and Bedwellty, for a lecturer to give sermons at Bedwellty
and Mynyddislwyn every three weeks, and for a Charity School.
He made provision for the erection of a school and for clothing
and apprenticing fifteen boys. The boys were dressed in blue
cloth and in 1809 we find the master complaining to the trustees
that very few Blue Boys are attending the school and that " the
few that attends (except two) are not capable of reading so much
as the Catechism."

73

Why precisely the young squire of Kilvach Vargoed should feel impelled to found a school for the poor boys of his own parish we do not know but many boys of the Rhymney Valley have reason to honour his memory. It has been suggested by Arthur Wright, the historian of the school, that Lewis may have been influenced by the philanthropic labours of the Rev. Thomas Gouge (1609-1681) in organising instruction in South Wales. The first mention of one of the circulating schools of Griffith Jones in Gelligaer is not until 1738.

The Lewis school was continued for a century in Gelligaer village. Afterwards buildings were erected on the present site at Pengam. Down to the year 1875 the school was conducted as a free elementary school. In April, 1875, it was converted into a secondary school under a new scheme, which was again modified after the passing of the Intermediate Education Act, 1889. In the meantime the value of the original bequest had been greatly enhanced by the sinking of coalpits.

I failed to win a scholarship but I was sent to the school, nevertheless, as a day-boy going to and fro by train daily. I think the fees were only two or three pounds per annum. There were two masters : David Evans, M.A.—we always added the M.A. for the reason, I believe, that he was the first Welshman, or one of the first, to win this degree at the University of London; and Roger W. Jones. He was then only a B.A., but as teacher he was superior to his chief. David Evans, an able Methodist minister from North Wales, was chosen out of eighty-three applicants. He had been trained at Borough Road College and at Bala College and was a frequent contributor to the Welsh periodical press. Now he was teaching small boys, " shampooing dull minds," a task for which he was not obviously fitted. He lacked patience, and had a mediaeval conception of corporal punishment.  His best work was a standard history of the Sunday Schools of Wales published in 1884.

Roger Jones laid stress on good manners.  His voice was quiet and one word spoken from him firmly and gravely would keep order throughout the day.  Weeks would pass in his class without the cane being produced.  He was infinitely encouraging when he saw signs of effort.  And he could teach.  That is to say, he knew how to awaken curiosity and kindle enthusiasm, how to give us a glimpse of Paradise.  Once this is done the student does the rest spontaneously.

There was throughout the school a strong bias against work, and every device to evade it was admired.  The better-off boarders hired the poorer boys to write out impositions and as these usually took the form of writing out the same word or sentence fifty or a hundred times we became expert in the use of two pencils at once.

Among the boarders who were my contemporaries was J. H. Davies, the son of a country squire from my father's native village, Llangeitho.  In 1919, Davies, then Registrar of the University College at Aberystwyth, and I met again as rival candidates for the Principalship.  He had behind him a fine record of bibliographical service to Welsh literature and of public work in the county and he had the backing of the college President, the distinguished physician, Sir John Williams, K.C.V.O.  I had none of these qualifications.  Davies beat me easily and even more easily the third candidate, a greater scholar than either of us, Sir John Edward Lloyd, F.B.A.

I played no games and could not learn to swim.  I tried cricket but I seemed always to be fielding and never to be given a chance to bat.  True when once given a chance I scored no runs. I fought once only with another boy and then had the wit in the middle of the scuffle to laugh at its absurdity and thus end it—probably thereby avoiding defeat.

Another contemporary was David W. Evans, who left for Llandovery and Oxford and later became Sir David and my successor in the direction of the work of the Welsh National Memorial Association for the Prevention of Tuberculosis, founded in 1912.

We were for the most part a rough and uncouth lot of loons and dolts and wrought not a little damage on the railway stock on our daily journeys. Of sexual indecencies in the school I remember nothing beyond a few filthy words and phrases chalked on the walls and doors of lavatories. The boarders were better dressed and better mannered than the day boys but not better scholars. I recall one mincing dandy who paraded in buckled knickerbockers and coloured stockings. Some lessons could at first be very bewildering to little Welsh boys. There were so many strange words: Vocative and Ablative, Indicative and Subjunctive, Orthography and Etymology, Syntax and Prosody. And in another classroom we encountered the mysteries of Euclid and Algebra and words like isosceles and hypotenuse. We were shown the how of Algebra but not the why of it. It may be today an exploded fallacy that some boys are congenitally bad at mathematics and good at classics, but teachers of mathematics producing correct solutions on a blackboard reminded me of conjurors producing rabbits out of a hat. To me there seemed obviously so many more wrong than right ways of doing a problem, and this infirmity was to pursue me for many years and ultimately to change the course of my life.

Latin was taught by the headmaster. We construed *De Bello Gallico* with incredible slowness. Between the lessons we had to memorize the vocabulary at the end of Dr. William Smith's *Principia Latina* learning columns of letter A one day, B the next day and so forth and promptly forgetting the words learnt yesterday for lack of exercising them.

My father was not a reader, except of the trade journals, the *Grocer* and the *Ironmonger*, until old age and retirement, so we had very few books at 100, High Street. Two or three books I remember besides the Bible and hymn book : the *Christian Instructor* and *Confession of Faith* ; the *Pilgrim's Progress*, the complete works of Williams Pantycelyn, and a history of the Welsh by Owen Jones, Manchester. All these were in Welsh. But at Pengam there was an old cupboard with books presented to the school by Charles Henry James, M.P. for Merthyr, and there under the guidance of Roger Jones I found salvation. "I shall light a candle of understanding in thine heart which shall not be put out." I began to read what might be called literaturè as distinct from the gilded volumes of the *Prize* or the *Children's Friend* presented to us at Christmas and the histories of Jack Sheppard and Charles Peace which I bought in endless penny numbers from the local stationer. At Pengam there was a small nondescript room, off the main class room, where the day-boys toasted rashers of bacon or sausages before an open fire for lunch. In a corner of this room there were books in the shabby and ricketty old cupboard which took a Rhymney boy away into the realms of wonder over the seas to the Malay Archipelago, to Abyssinia, to the sources of the Nile and the Albert Nyanza, to the curiosities of natural history, piloted by James Bruce, Samuel Baker, and Frank Buckland. And it was during these Pengam days, to escape the disturbance caused by the birth of one or other of my recurring brothers and sisters, that I was sent out of the way to stay at my grandfather's house at Penuel Row, and in a sitting room upstairs I struck a goldmine in the shape of a finely illustrated set of volumes containing the story of the travellers who had gone in search of the North and South Poles and of the North West Passage : the Cabots, Willoughby, Frobisher, John Davies, Hudson, down to the voyages of Sir John Franklin and Parry and Ross in the nineteenth century— exciting stories of heroic endeavour against tremendous odds. Volumes of this sort, some in Welsh, were usually printed in Edinburgh and bought in Rhymney on the instalment system from itinerant booksellers.

Roger Jones infected me with a love of reading. He contrived to convey to his pupil his own passionate interest in some particular book. He professed to be astounded, shocked, distressed, to discover that I had lived to be thirteen without having read Macaulay's essays on Clive and Warren Hastings. What had I been doing with my time ? So I secured a copy, a double-columned fat edition, of all the essays from Dobbin's shop in Cardiff for two shillings or half a crown. Before this I had been given five shillings by my mother for passing some examination. I went up to the village book-shop and asked Johnny Capel to go through his catalogues till he found a history book which cost five shillings and order it. It turned out to be Pinnock's *History of England* which I recall for the passages of poetry which prefaced each chapter. William Pinnock and his son William Henry Pinnock, both now quite forgotten, were amongst the most influential authors of Victorian England, and a list of their works fills seven columns of the British Museum catalogue. The book which luck brought me was an abridgement of Goldsmith's *History of England*. It ran into scores of editions and had for frontispiece portraits of the idols of the

Ancient Britons and Saxons. Thor was seated on a throne
like a chaired bard at an Eisteddfod. At the head of the chapter
on Victoria's accession was the verse :

> They deck'd her courtly halls—
> They rein'd her hundred steeds ;
> They shouted at her palace gate
> ' A noble queen succeeds.'

We wrote on the fly leaves of books which belonged to
us rhymes which had come down from previous centuries
when books were scarce and valued :

> Dinah Jones is my name,
> England is my nation,
> Rhymney is my dwelling place,
> And Christ is my salvation.
> When I am dead and in my grave
> And all my bones are rotten
> This little book will tell my name
> When others are forgotten.

Which reminds me of another jingle popular with children :

> Crawshay Bailey had an engine,
> She was puffing and a blowing,
> She could go ten miles an hour
> And go faster if you shoved her.
>   Did you ever see
>   Such a funny thing before ?

Quiet to read for a studious member of a numerous and
growing family is a perennial problem. The Terrace, to which
we moved from High Street when I was aged eleven, was
a row of superior houses where the managers lived. The
houses were graded to correspond to the industrial importance
of their occupants. At each end was a large house standing

in its own walled-in grounds with trees and garden to match ; these were occupied by the manager of the Company Shop and the chief colliery manager. Then next to these came at each end a house of intermediate size, one occupied by the cashier and one by the assistant-general-manager ; the rest of the row was filled in with houses half in size of the two intermediaries, for the lesser managers or superior foremen. We first moved to an ordinary and then to an intermediate, which had ample accommodation. The removal was a proof that my father's position in the Company Shop was improving. He was no longer an assistant but a manager of sorts. The inhabitants of the Terrace did not form a coherent society in virtue of their proximity. We were good neighbours but we never took tea at either of the end houses while we lived in an ordinary. They were Church and we were Chapel—that formed an effective social barrier. We did not then speak of the bourgeoisie and proletariat.

The Terrace had lines of railway running before and behind it and periodically when shipments of pitwood arrived from Norway the cargo was tipped higgledy piggledy out of the trucks alongside the railway at the end of the row and left there for months. There would be many thousands of props about six feet long. The son of the roller-man and I solved the problem of quiet for a time by constructing a passage leading to a secret cave in the alluring recesses of the mountain of pitwood, into the depths of which we retreated with our dreams and a horn lamp and candle. Crouching in the semi-light we read Fenimore Cooper and other authors and fancied ourselves Indians. But we were never quite free of the fear of detection and we did not in fact get much reading done. We thought our lot a hard one and we toyed with the notion of emigrating to Manitoba. Shipping agents were flooding the valley with Canadian propaganda—pictures of rolling plains of golden corn. Settlers were offered 160 acres of land on the same terms as the gospel—without money and without price—on the Western Prairies. Once there miles and miles from everybody we should be able to read night and day without interruption. We hummed together some lines I had heard my mother sing :

Here we had toil and little to reward it,
But there shall plenty smile upon our pain,
And ours shall be the mountain and the forest,
And boundless prairies ripe with golden grain.
Cheer boys, Cheer, for England, mother England,
Cheer boys, Cheer, united heart and hand,
Cheer boys, Cheer, there's wealth for honest labour,
Cheer boys, Cheer, in the new and happy land.

A year or two later, when I had begun to earn wages, I took train on a Saturday afternoon to Pontsarn to luxuriate in its silent woods and to finish reading *Far from the Madding Crowd*, without interruption. On other occasions I borrowed the key of Brynhyfryd on a week day and seated alone in the empty chapel read in perfect peace. "For unto you is Paradise opened, the tree of life is planted, the time to come is prepared, plenteousness is made ready."

# CHAPTER VI

## Minor Miseries

*Chommoda dicebat, si quando commoda vellet
Dicere, et hinsidias Arrius insidias.*

Catullus.

I HAVE one complaint to make of all my schoolmasters : they
did not impress upon me the importance of a correct treatment of the aspirate ; they did not tell me that the use and
misuse of this silent or sounded letter had for centuries divided
society into two parts and that the possession of a very large
income was required to ensure forgiveness for an offence.
Ruskin noticed this class barrier : " They liked, as they did
not drop their own *h*'s, to talk with people who did not drop
theirs." Men have had trouble with this sound from the days
of the Ephraimites as set forth in the Book of Judges. And
not only in these ancient days but I gather that much later,
in the days of the Romans, there are Latin inscriptions which
betray a variety of practice, where for example we may sometimes read *omo* and sometimes *hornamentum*. A learned student
of these matters, the Rev. Geoffrey Hill, points out that Catullus,
who moved in the best society in Rome, ridicules Arrius who
by a strange coincidence occupied the same position in the
poet's mind as the London 'Arry and 'Arriet do in English
life.

In the days of St. Augustine the proper use of the aspirate
continued to be a test of good breeding and from the first book

of the *Confessions* we learn that the man who dropped his *h's*
and decapitated human into 'uman offended society more than
if he committed murder. Fifteen hundred years later, in the
age of Victoria, an English Dean declares with appropriate
clerical dogmatism, that nothing so surely stamps a man as
below the mark in intelligence, self-respect, and energy as the
misuse of the aspirate. This is sweeping and I would plead
extenuating circumstances. Inheritance may have played a
part and environment most certainly did and should share
the guilt and condemnation. Learned authorities point to
historical and geographical origins :

> " We see districts where it is never improperly either
> put on or thrown aside, others where it is never used under
> any circumstances, others where it is dropped but never
> put on, and others again where it is put on and taken off ;
> and if we consult a map of England under the Heptarchy
> we shall see that these districts are to a great extent the
> same as some of the early Kingdoms."

I divide the blame between Monmouthshire and my early
preceptors. I was not warned. And for Monmouthshire
it may be pleaded that it marches with a part of England where
the dialect spoken by the English inhabitants does not possess
a single ' *h* '. A distinguished native of the county had the
wit to convert the blemish into a political and social asset and
to make it a cause of wit in others. When J. H. Thomas com-
plained to F. E. Smith that he had " an 'ell of an 'eadache "
the Lord Chancellor prescribed " a couple of aspirates." I did
not discover my geographical handicap until I went to college.
Thoroughbred Welshmen at Aberystwyth had no trouble with
the aspirate and they manipulated the initial and the medial
breathing with an unconscious ease which I could only envy

and aspire to with hard labour. Houyhnhnms and Yahoos had no terrors for them. I have corrected my intelligence and recovered my self-respect and am now apt to fall down only on the Dean's third count for I still sometimes lapse into omission when fatigued. The price of respectability is eternal vigilance. I had to come to London to learn of a newly created knight who was overheard on the telephone speaking to his brother : " Is that you 'Erb. This is Sir Hedward."

It may be conceded that the abuse of a single letter of the alphabet has stood in the way of a classless society but a much greater obstacle to unity and brotherly love has been the absence of spring cleaning in the home. What I have suffered from the letter ' h ' has been negligible compared with the torture and torment, the loss of time and temper, attributable to the furtive and flighty flea. It is one of the mysteries of human existence and divine justice that I should suffer and my neighbour be immune and if I thought any light would be thrown on the problem as a result I would willingly bequeath my body to a scientific institute of dermatology.

The subject is frequently mentioned in the literature of travel. Kinglake, it will be remembered, warned his readers against attempting to sleep in a holy city. In Tiberias, one of the four holy cities of the Jews, he encountered the fleas of all nations, " a carnal, self-seeking congregation." I have had the same experience in the holy city of Fez. A scorched skin and throbbing temples deprive the traveller of the spirit of devotion appropriate to his sacred surroundings.

Rhymney was and is a more salubrious place than Tiberias or Fez. A large proportion of the houses of the miners were spotlessly kept, and at 100, High Street I seemed always to be in the way of spring cleaning. But there were exceptions, and on these occasions a visit to a neighbour's house had to be abruptly terminated on some improvised excuse. A direct mention of the real reason would cause an even more painful and general sensation than that caused by the insect itself. And escape in the night was not always possible. Once in Cardiff I got out of bed and lay on the boards between the sheets of the *British Weekly* and the *Christian World*. On another occasion after a Sunday night I spread out row upon row on a half sheet of notepaper, twenty-three corpses, slain in twenty-three single combats, all through the night. I left the dead on the dressing table to tell their own tale to my hostess, after my departure on Monday morning.

You cannot take hold of a flea by the neck nor by the waist for it has neither and its jumping prowess always defeated my unaided fingers. A human flea (there are fifty kinds to be found in Great Britain alone) has been known to reach a height of $7\frac{3}{4}$ inches and to cover, besides, thirteen inches horizontally, equivalent to a leap of 300 yards by a six foot man. I went hunting armed with a damped cake of soap and conquest was followed by exhumation and vindictive stabbing at the point of the pin.

In South Wales I was a stranger to bugs and my first sight of one was in London when sharing a bed with a snoring companion and was myself nearly driven crazy. It was not open to me to do as the saints do in such situations. Their technique is set out in the *Acts of John* translated by Dr. M. R. James and quoted by Mr. Charlesworth in *Five Men*.

'I say unto you, O bugs, behave yourselves, one and all and leave your abode for this night and remain quiet in one place, and keep your distance from the servants of God.' And as we laughed and went on talking for some time, John addressed himself to sleep; and we, talking low, thanks to him were not disturbed.

I woke my companion in South London and said that I had heard that Covent Garden was a wonderful sight at three in the morning. I dared not tell him the truth—it was his home. He turned over and was asleep at once. I crept out into the street and walked miles to Covent Garden where I found a coffee stall open and recovered my sanity. I never returned to that bed. During this visit I heard Joseph Parker preach at the City Temple, and Benjamin Jowett preach on John Wesley in Westminster Abbey.

Whether the birth-rate among fleas is falling throughout Europe I am not sure; it is I think the fact in the Scandinavian countries, in Germany and in Switzerland, where, as I was once told by a native of Appenzell, " cleanliness is our speciality." I have read of a campaign for their extermination in Soviet Russia. Thanks primarily to the London County Council and to the London Passenger Transport Board the flea population of the metropolis is today far less than when I first came up to London from the country. I cannot quote precise statistics but I can now travel in trams and tubes and buses unmolested, a rare experience in the dirty nineties. It will always be a matter of regret to me that the name of Keating has not appeared in an Honours list.

ALLTDDU, TREGARON

GWYNFIL, LLANGEITHO

# CHAPTER VII

## HOLIDAYS

*O olwg hagrwch Cynnydd*
  *A thrist domenni'r gwaith,*
*Mae bro rhwng môr a mynydd*
  *Heb arni staen na chraith,*
*Ond lle bu'r aradr ar y ffridd*
*Yn rhwygo'r gwanwyn pêr o'r pridd.*
R. WILLIAMS PARRY.

*Beyond the mounds and litter*
  *Man's progress and man's hand,*
*Between mountain and water*
  *A stainless, unscarred land ;*
*And there the plough in its upland toil*
*Will plough the Spring from the furrowed soil.*
Trans. by DAVID BELL.

THE thriftier elements of the population went for a week or a fortnight's holiday in the summer to one of the mineral springs in Mid Wales—Llanwrtyd or Builth Wells ; some went to the seaside at the Mumbles, Llanstephan, Aberaeron or Aberystwyth. The rest had to be content with a day trip on the Channel to Weston-Super-Mare or Ilfracombe or with a Sunday School picnic.

The first of such holidays which I recall was to Swansea where our mother and children stayed in stuffy lodgings near the beach in Rodney Street, a name which surprised me as rodney was our term for a down-at-heel wastrel. It had a certain fitness. It was a shabby street. We paid the landlady for " rooms and attendance " and bought our provisions in minute quantities. I can still smell the musty-fusty cupboard in which they were stored, and see the brownish wallpaper with a damp patch on the weather side of the parlour which served us as sitting and dining room.

I once went for a short stay to Cardiff and one day wandered out to some fields in Roath, not then built upon, where some donkeys were straying. I had a precious whip, its handle ending in a sheep's foot, one of my father's presents from Bristol. A smart street gamin came up and offered to catch a donkey for me if I would lend him the whip. I did so and when he scampered off and never returned I realised he had already caught one donkey.

One other aspect of life I discovered when sent to the Rhondda to stay at a public house with relatives who kept it. There I saw the same few colliers " on the spree " soaking themselves in drink day after day for the week I was there. My education was proceeding. On an earlier holiday in Cardiganshire our mother had brought back a lad for whom my father found a job in the drapery section of the Company Shop. He came from a farm midway between Tregaron and Pont-rhydfendigaid and to this farm I was sent for several years in succession with a younger brother. It was called Alltddu. My father gave me a pocketbook in which I wrote the name of each railway station from Rhymney to Tregaron. On one of these journeys the collector at Lampeter asked for our tickets. I had forgotten that I had put them in my hat band, as I had seen others do. There was panic for a moment until the collector spied them. Many years later I read Hardy's poem:

" In the band of his hat the journeying boy
  Had a ticket stuck ; and a string
  Around his neck bore the key of his box,
  That twinkled gleams of the lamp's sad beams
  Like a living thing."

On my arrival I insisted on adding to the list of stations
in the precious pocketbook the names of the farms for miles
around Alltddu, a lesson in Welsh orthography. I still remember
many of them : Maeselwad, Maesllyn, Bronmwyn, Bryncipyll,
Yr Hen Fynachlog, Mynachlog Fawr, Camer, Cruglas, Y Fedw,
Glanbrenig, Tre-cefel, Nant-coy, Brynhoewnant. The horses
and dogs had English names, the cows Welsh. The fields
had each a Welsh name : Cae'r Odyn, Cae Pistyll, Cae Lloi
and so forth. It was a farm of some hundred and sixty acres
with one hundred acres of sheep walk and two hundred and
fifty acres of peat bog and thirty acres of woodland. It was
rented from the Earl of Lisburne, the house standing between the
the main road and the railway which runs from Lampeter to
Aberystwyth, three miles from Tregaron and alongside the
extensive peat bog. The infrequent trains which passed did
not seriously diminish the sense of solitude. Letters had to
be fetched from Tregaron.

The household consisted of the venerable father, no longer
active, two sons and two daughters, all grown up, unmarried
and occupied in the house and on the land. In addition there
was a married ploughman in a near-by cottage, and a maid
servant. All were astir daily at five o'clock, family prayers
and breakfast followed at eight, dinner at noon, supper at seven,
family prayers and bed at nine. This routine was disturbed
for the market at Tregaron on Tuesdays and for the chapel

services on Sundays. To these we usually drove in a trap, which could seat five. Occasionally I rode pillion with Miss James on the back of the best mare *Derby*. On Sundays I was left in Tregaron for the day in the house of the local registrar, where there was fresh meat for dinner. At the farm the food was plentiful but rather monotonous. A fat cow was killed and salted and the mid-day meal usually consisted of boiled pickled beef, bacon and potatoes. This was varied with a rabbit. Broth was provided half an hour before dinner when the men were working near the house. It was served in wooden bowls and each had his or her wooden spoon. I was given an egg as a breakfast treat, the others had flummery. Bread was home-baked. Peat supplied the firing on the broad hearth under a chimney wide open to the heavens. Each farm had an allotted portion of the bog and there the peat was geometrically cut—killed, in Welsh—and stacked, dried and harvested. The best clothes were homespun ; cheap cottons, wallpaper and earthenware were picked up at the monthly fair from yelling English hawkers. The father, a deacon, went to chapel in whipcord breeches and brown gaiters. There were no sanitary arrangements within or without the farmhouses in those days.

There was always something worth while to do about the farm and I was proud to be allowed to help. I could fetch the cattle for the milking, armed with a stick twice my height, calling the cows by their names : Seren, Penwen and so forth. I could feed the acrobatic calves, mostly legs, and let them bang their silly noses against the cans in their determination to lick the last drop. On wet days in the barn I could paint the gambo red, polish the harness or twist ropes of straw for thatching by means of a simple turnstick. Or I could take short spells at the churn in the clean cool dairy with its big slab of slate and wide shallow pans, while listening to the elusive corncrake calling in the meadow outside.

Far in the Plinlimmon mountains are three or four farms where the shearing of thousands of sheep is a matter for the co-operation of the whole countryside. Every summer the sons and daughters of the Vale of Teify ride up to help and spend two or three days in the mountains joyously working, feasting and frolicking, and then they race their ponies home again. Or they did when I was a boy at Alltddu in the early eighties.

It is the fashion to poke fun at the characteristics of the small peasantry of the type I am describing, their cupidity, their indifference to beauty, their narrow interests and self-deception. My memory may be treacherous, or my experience may have been exceptional, but the life of the family with whom I lived in close intimacy if narrow in outlook was neither sordid nor hypocritical. It was transfigured by the graceful acts and thousand decencies of daily life ; the gentler virtues softened and hallowed the hard toil of the fields, and the home had a simple beauty which in retrospect I find difficult to parallel in my subsequent experience.

Doubtless there lingered in the neighbourhood less pleasant things which were hidden from the eyes of childhood and which religion had failed to extirpate. As late as 1803 a clerical visitor to this very district could write :—

> " The mode of courtship, and the ceremony of the little wedding we noticed in North Wales, obtains here ; but some more attention has been paid to religion ; they have been taught the criminality of having a community of wives, as well as been convinced of its unreasonableness and impolicy ; so that this outrage upon order and decency begins rapidly to subside."

Perhaps I read into the domestic life at Alltddu something of the beauty of the natural scene which surrounded it.
Wherever I have gone I have taken with me the memory of
a small boy resting on a field-gate at eventide, gazing across the
outspread marsh towards the dark waters of the Teify, across
the polished surfaces of the peat pools, fluttered by snipe and
teal, the trees on the bank behind him settling down to rest
for the night, drawing their leaves closer together in the waning
light. The sun sinks, the colours of the landscape fade into
each other; the blades of grass and the tops of the cotton plant
tremble and shiver in the cool breeze which creeps over the
bog as the sun sets. Night falls and the small boy 'full of
sweet desolation', is put to bed and all he remembers after
that is turning over in his sleep as the last train roars on its
way homewards to Aberystwyth between nine and ten o'clock.

One other evening memory recurs to me. I had gone
up the lane which led to a hill above the house to gather fern
for bedding and having filled my sack I was resting, poetically,
'along a shelving bank of turf' by a stream and mingling my
thoughts with 'the sound of waters murmuring' when I became
suddenly aware of a sinister presence standing over me. It was
the alien gamekeeper with his malevolent gaze fixed on me.
He thought I was poaching. He looked into the sack. I was
innocent but stiff with terror. Fifty years later, when staying
overnight at Trawscoed as the guest of Lord Lisburne and
looking over with him the plans of the Alltddu farm buildings
and fields I had the belated satisfaction of cursing his father's
gamekeeper.

# CHAPTER VIII

## Work and Wages

*Chimney stacks of all dimensions*
*Send their curling smoke on high*
*To fulfil divine intentions*
*And make heaven's rich drapery.*

Local Rhymer, 1889.

I HAD to leave Pengam in my fourteenth year much against my will. I had passed the Cambridge Local and finished up second in the school at the summer examination conducted by the Cambridge Syndics. I wrote hither and thither for prospectuses of colleges like Llandovery and Brecon, which prepared boys for the Universities, but my grandfather was firm and declared that I had had enough of schooling and that it was time I entered " the university of real life " as he put it. Already I had often helped my father by getting up at four o'clock on Saturday mornings and going with him in the dark, feeling very important, to the Company Shop where I wrote labels with addresses of customers, weights and values, and dabbed them on pieces of meat which my father and the butchers cut up in the slaughter house in accordance with the orders collected from customers on Friday. The butchers killed five or six beasts, ten or twelve porkers, and from twenty to thirty sheep every week. We chopped them into small pieces in the early hours of Saturday ready to be delivered for Sunday's dinner—the high feast of the workman's week.

Immediately after leaving Pengam I was found a temporary job as timekeeper on the Company's farm near where Maclaren's Pit and Abertysswg village now stand. A squad of eight or ten men came every summer from Breconshire and beyond to scythe the grass in the two great fields which ran for a mile above and below the Brecon and Merthyr Railway. Local women and girls came to harvest the hay, perhaps forty or fifty of them. I had a small pony to help me along. This was a holiday post.

My first regular job was also that of timekeeper, but now in the " Works." The works of the Rhymney Iron Company Limited sprawled over the right and left bank of the river on the level land whereas the pit shafts, for the most part, stood against the sky on the hillsides. The works consisted of blast furnaces and Bessemer plant for the conversion of iron ore into steel and of mills for turning the same into bars and rails, sleepers and fishplates. In addition there was a series of ' shops ' which danced attendance on the productive plant and a series of offices for the clerical staff. I began in the Time Office under the Chief Engineer, John Rees Williams, who superintended the ' shops '. He entered my name in a book with twelve shillings per week over against it. It then went to the Chief Cashier and came back in due course with the twelve shillings struck out and nine shillings substituted. I think this was the only wage reduction I suffered until the Geddes axe fell upon all Civil Servants in 1922. In addition to my duties as timekeeper I had to make fair copies of specifications of plant ordered for the shops, and I thus became familiar with engineering terminology and with the names of prominent contractors like Bayliss Jones and Bayliss, and Babcock and Willcox.

In the Time Office there was at one end a glazed passage, with one pane taken out. Before the inside window stood an oblong table divided into eight hundred receptacles each holding three numbered metal tokens, about an inch and an eighth in diameter. At six a.m. each man was given three discs with his own number on, and he returned them at 8-15 a.m., 1 and 6 p.m. respectively. The men came rushing through the passage in the last minutes before the six o'clock hooter blew so that I learnt to deal out the discs with great rapidity hardly glancing at the table before me. I felt rather like Paderewski at the piano keys. I had to check this record by visiting the shops with a notebook three times a day. On my return, seated on an a high stool I put a stroke against each person's name in a folio as big as myself. Cassell's National Library was coming out then in threepenny volumes, one a week, and one day the manager caught me reading one of them. I used to keep the little book open between the leaves of the big ledger and turn the large leaves over quickly when disturbed. Instead of blaming me the manager encouraged me and brought me books of his own, among them three by Samuel Smiles : *Self Help*, *Character*, and *Lives of the Engineers*. I was urged to learn shorthand, which I did well enough to earn Pitman's certificate for a moderate speed. What John Rees Williams did for me I have since tried to do for those who have worked in offices with me—given them books, and urged them to read them in office hours if there was no work to do.

I had left school but I was not done with study or with ambition. No doubt I was a horrid little prig. I drew up a scheme of study, one of many, and sent it to Roger Jones at Pengam. He gave me wise advice and encouragement. *Inter alia* he warned me of the perils of what I should now call calf love, but I regret to say that to his warnings on this painful subject I gave no heed. My day at the works lasted from 5-45 a.m. till 6-45 p.m., and on Monday and Thursday evenings there were services at our chapel which I was expected to attend and did attend regularly. My mother let me have a small sitting-room to myself and for the next five years I spent my limited leisure in it reading far into the night, and nights of enchantment they were. What is there in adult life comparable with the excitement of the developing mind of youth, embarking on the wide domain of knowledge, spurred to strain every sinew by the restriction of opportunity and the poverty of equipment ?

A Pengam boy known to me was reading for a Civil Service examination and he encouraged me to do likewise, lending me books and helping me in many ways. I had some postal preparation from an Edinburgh firm, on whose staff was a tutor whose name amused me—Chuckerbutty. Candidates for Lower Division Clerkships were weeded out in a preliminary examination. I sat in Cardiff and in January 1887 a large blue (not buff) envelope arrived, inscribed by Horace Mann, ' acquainting ' me that I had passed. I toiled away at Book-keeping, Digesting Returns, Indexing, Arithmetic and in trying to make my handwriting conform to the standard civil service pattern. Someone in Parliament grumbled at the Civil Service Estimates and Lord Randolph Churchill appointed a Royal Commission. The competitive examination was postponed time and again and I never sat it. Meanwhile my Pengam friend, James Evans, had been assigned to the Irish Land Commission in Dublin where he was employed from 10 to 4 calculating percentages of reductions in Irish produce for the previous six years, by which percentages the judges of the Commission were guided in reducing rents. He rose later to be His Majesty's Chief Poor Law Inspector for Wales and on his retirement from the Service was chosen chairman of the Rhondda tribunal under the Unemployment Assistance Board.

At some date in the late eighties I was promoted from the Time Office to the Forge and Mill Office. This office, under the Mill manager, was concerned with executing the orders for steel rails, bars, sleepers, and fishplates, sent down from the London office of the Company, with their inspection and despatch, with invoicing them, and also with the engagement and dismissal of workmen, their time and pay. I shared in both branches but at first mainly, once more, in timekeeping. There was a timekeeper much my senior, Robert Thomas, familiarly known as " Robin bach ", owing to his small size. He had taken shorthand up to the reporting stage, and he was a first rate public speaker ; he always knew his case and could put it clearly. As he was a convinced and fearless nonconformist he was a marked man in the community but it was so difficult to find any fault with his work that it took quite a long time to eliminate him. I looked up to him as our village Abdiel " unshaken, unseduced, unterrified."

Robert Thomas played a valiant part in the prolonged struggle for and against the consecration of the new public cemetery which was waged in 1884. The Local Board had applied to Whitehall and obtained powers to borrow £2,500. Lord Bute, from whom the land was to be obtained, required that a part of the ground should be apportioned to the Roman Catholics and a portion to the Church of England. The Clerk of the Board gave it as his opinion that if ground were consecrated the Board would be compelled to provide a chapel. This was confirmed by learned Counsel and it was laid down that the consecrated portion could be used only for performance of burials according to the rites of the Established Church.

A fierce controversy followed in the Press and in public meetings. It turned largely on Scripture precedents. Where was Moses buried ? There was no account given in the Bible of the consecration of the grave by any outward form ; the same was true of David's grave, and of the grave of our Lord.

It was carried at the Board by one vote that the ground be divided into three parts for burials according to the rites of the Established Church, the Roman Catholic Church, and the nonconformists respectively. Meanwhile an election took place amid great excitement. The three retiring candidates were defeated and three nonconformists were elected in their place. But one of these voted for consecration—none other than my Time Office chief, John Rees Williams. So the motion in favour of consecration was once again carried by one vote. Thereafter the dead were buried in peace, this body in holy ground and that body in common clay.

The rest of the Mill Office staff included two seniors, one an Anglican and the other a Baptist, and a junior who was also a churchman. We were an efficient team and the work went so smoothly that we found frequent opportunity for disputation. One topic was uppermost—the disestablishment of the Welsh Church. The other junior and I were the chief disputants, our elders being more cautious. The argument did not move on the highest levels—it largely revolved around the absurdity of apostolical succession, the marital history of Henry the Eighth and the more scabrous stories in the annals of church and clergy. We bandied statistics of the strength or weakness of the established church compared with the various denominations and I was not a little disconcerted when, as not infrequently happened, some nonconformist minister " who affected to step into the spiritualities of the Church of England " did actually step into its temporalities. Commenting publicly on one of these turncoats a local orator declared : " Napoleon quitted his throne, and now the Reverend W. P. Davies has quitted his and gone into exile in the State Church." On the other hand, my opponent argued that dissenters were heretics, schismatics, idolators. Dissatisfied with the true church, planted in Jerusalem in apostolic times, they had like Jeroboam, the son of Nebat, gone forth to Dan and Bethel and set up calves of gold, and made priests from among all the people which were not the sons of Levi. And so the war of texts went on interminably.

The workmen employed in the steel mills, for the most part, were of an inferior social grade to the artisans with whom I had dealt in the Time Office. The roughers and rollers, it is true, earned far more money than the mechanics ; they were on piece work and their wages might rise to seven or eight pounds in a week. They were men of strength and skill handling heavy white-hot ingots and consuming enormous quantities of liquid. But the rank and file, men and women, were unskilled and did not make a pound a week. Many were Irish, earning fourteen shillings and even so they would lose a quarter now and again in the morning, or succumb to the attraction of the Rock Inn or the Bute Arms in the afternoon.

My single appearance in a police court was to give evidence in Merthyr against a man who had gone off to the Rock or the Bute and left untended, and thus ruined, a furnace charged with ingots. These inns were planted in a district called Sodom and Gomorrah. I was more frightened than the prisoner by the mechanical procedure of the court. The prisoner was jerked into the dock by a policeman ; I was jerked into the witness box ; a lawyer bobbed up here, another bobbed up there, a clerk whispered to the Stipendiary and the case was over before I realized it had begun.

My day now began at nine and finished at seven after I had gone the round of the night shift. I used the new freedom of the early morning to go with another clerk, Henry Lewis, to New-town pond, not to bathe in its waters, but to walk on its banks, committing poetry to memory. There were two poets who appealed to Victorian adolescents of the earnest evangelical type, Phillip James Bailey, the author of *Festus* and Robert Pollock, the author of the *Course of Time*. Both were Glasgow students and very nearly contemporaries. Both wrote their masterpieces in their early twenties in blank verse, both were immensely popular in their day and are now forgotten. The one poem was drenched in Calvinism, the other in optimism. Robert Pollock was a divinity student and died of tuberculosis in 1827 before he was thirty. I remember his description of Byron : "Drank every cup of joy, heard every trump of fame, drank early, deeply drank, drank draughts that common millions might have quenched—then died of thirst because there was no more to drink." *Festus* was published when the author was twenty-three. It contains some twenty thousand lines, four of which are still quoted :

" We live in deeds, not years, in thoughts, not breaths,
    In feelings, not in figures on a dial,
    We should count time by heart-throbs. He most lives
    Who thinks most, feels the noblest, acts the best."

In 1901, seventy years after the publication of his poem and within a year of his death, Bailey was made an honorary LL.D. of his old university.

Harry Lewis and I sleeked our tongues in the upland morning air shouting Calvinistic theology in blank verse. Truth requires that I should add that in our morning recitals we mingled passages from Wordsworth, Shelley and Keats from the weekly numbers of *Great Thoughts*. Men pent in offices, or in cities bound, find relief in singing and shouting. Who has not halloaed to the reverberate hills or out-sung Caruso alone in a railway compartment ? I have enjoyed myself singing aloud unheard Welsh hymns in the roar of London's traffic. An American poet has told me that he once bought a batch of evening papers from a newsboy in order to have the exhilaration of running shouting through the streets of New York.

Lewis was a pay-clerk so expert that he could add up the shillings and pence columns together, and could tell without reckoning whether his hand held nineteen, twenty, or twenty-one shillings. Threatened with consumption he migrated to South Africa where he became a book-keeper to a firm of ostrich feather merchants at £12 10s. a month and later an accountant. I succeeded him in Rhymney as auditor of the Rechabite Society. Before he left home we debated publicly with the audacity of ignorant youth Creation versus Evolution. He confessed to me afterwards that he had written for guidance in defending Evolution to a then well-known divine and Gilchrist lecturer, whom I had heard lecture in Dowlais for a penny on the *Infinitely Great and the Infinitely Little in Nature.* He was Dr. W. H. Dallinger and this is what he wrote to Lewis.:

" It is not easy, if it be possible to ' get up ' a preparation for such a discussion as you speak of. You are on the right side if you know how to hold your position. You must first

(1)   Show that Evolution as taught by Darwin is a fact
      in Nature.  For this purpose read the *Origin of Species*
      of Darwin with great care.  Also the *Scientific Evidences
      of Organic Evolution* by G. Romanes.  Published by
      Macmillan.  Also Darwin's *Life* by T. Bettany, B.SC.

(2)   You must show that there is an Evolution taught
      (by Haeckel and even Herbert Spencer) that is false
      as well as non-Theistic, but that Darwin's *Origin of
      Species* is the interpretation of the facts of nature and
      a gain to Theism and Religion.  The only books
      of the kind you ask for that I know of are, 1.  *A
      Defence of Philosophic Doubt* by A. Balfour.  2, *The
      Philosophy of Religion* and 3, *The Creator* by myself,
      published by Woolmer, 2 Castle Street, City Road,
      London.

      This last has a direct bearing on your wants and may
      be obtained for 1s. 6d."

The rollerman's son, already mentioned, after serving
an apprenticeship as a mechanic, went to Barry as an improver,
earning 24s. a week, when journeymen earned 36s.  He paid
14s. a week for his board and lodging, sharing a bed with another
mechanic and the sitting room with three others.  This con-
gestion drove him to sea as a third engineer at £7 a month.
He finished up as a publican, an occupation which enabled
him to retire quite early in life and he is now a faithful member
of the Church in Wales.

My duties at the Mill Office embraced invoicing orders
and copying letters in the old fashioned hand presses still to
be found in lawyers' offices.  For the invoices we used carbon
papers making a copy for the London office, a copy for the
buyers, and retained one ourselves.

Workmen were not paid their wages in full at the end of the week or as was usual at the end of the week following that in which the wages had been earned. A portion of the whole was retained by the Company and paid in a lump periodically. I shall explain this system more fully when I come to write of the Company Shop. A final settlement might not take place for seven or nine or even, as I remember on one occasion, twenty four weeks. The settlement days were known as Pay Saturdays and the week before as Turnbooks. On these occasions at the Mill Office we worked through the Friday night in order to calculate each workman's pay, the advances, and the amount due to him. All had to be exactly balanced and woe to the clerk guilty of the smallest error, for a penny out might hold us up for hours.

My own dominant interests by this time were far removed from such routine clerical work. No foreman can chain the mind of youth. But I cannot pretend that my job bored me. It did not. There was always the human interest beyond the names and figures in the ledgers. I knew every man and woman in the mills and on the banks. My bent for books was balanced by a bent for people and the steel mills provided a sample of the sorts and conditions which compose mankind. The rollers and roughers, the heaters and hookers-in, the wheelers and picklers of the time-books were also John Jones, Bill Smith, or Pat Murphy. There were scroungers and scrimshankers among them, no doubt, but that did not make them less interesting. Pat Murphy, for instance, had a leg of timber. Whether this infirmity made him indisposed to do a full day's work I do not know, but there were Saturdays when after drawing his miserable pay his wife Joanna thought the amount inadequate and she would visit the office to tell us so, calling at the Bute

Arms on the way. The old harridan would arrive with clenched fist crying and cursing, mad with spirits, clawing the air in her fury, and would hiss a stream of invective at us, singly and collectively, with a blasting vocabulary comparable only to the comprehensive curse of Ernulphus the Bishop, supplied to Mr. Shandy by the chapter clerk of the dean and chapter of Rochester, or Southey's Aballiboozabanganorribo.

Occasionally a misfit or ne'er-do-well would vanish from the mill and I would learn that he had joined the militia and gone into training at the barracks in Brecon. In an incredibly short time the lousy loafer would come back changed into an upstanding masher, scrubbed and shaved and tailored, swaggering along the High Street in his red coat, swishing his cane, the cynosure of all eyes, for a soldier was almost as rare amongst us as a whistling bishop.

My next promotion was to the Cashier's Office, after the office of the General Manager, the most coveted. I was now done with time-keeping. In this place ruled a chief-cashier whom we called the British Lion either because he sang a song with that title or because of his broad chest, rosy cheeks and flowing reddish brown hair and beard—I forget which. We sat on high stools opposite each other at the same high desk which sloped towards each of us. The calculations here were more advanced than in the other offices and included problems in what we called Mensuration. The Lion would shout each problem at me, doing the sum himself as well. He was at first faster than I was and as soon as he had got his result he paced up and down the room now humming lightly, now roaring galumphantly, and of course making it much harder for me to reach a correct solution. But it was all good-humoured and part of the university training prescribed by my grandfather.

# CHAPTER IX

## The Company Shop

*The propensity to truck, barter, and exchange one thing for another . . . . is common to all men, and to be found in no other race of animals.*

Adam Smith.

THE Rhymney Iron Co. had its head office in London with a chairman, a board of directors, and a secretary all resident outside Wales. Orders from customers for the Works were obtained in London and sent to Rhymney to be executed. The rivalry between the local Companies was intense and there was one in each valley engaged in identical manufacture : Blaenavon, Ebbw Vale, Tredegar, Rhymney, Dowlais. It was the era of wasteful unmitigated competition, before any attempt had been made to aggregate capital, concentrate control, and specialise production.

The chairman of the Rhymney Company during my youth was Sir Henry Tyler, M.P. Born in 1827, he was now a venerable figure with a domed head and an ample, flowing beard. He had been an Inspector of Railways at the Board of Trade but had left the Service for the more lucrative rewards of private business and freedom to write to the *Quarterly Review*. In due course he became chairman of thirteen companies in three continents. Whether they were more prosperous than the Rhymney Company I do not know. For eighteen years he controlled the Grand Trunk Railway of Canada " with results of a somewhat chequered complexion." A similar understatement might be applied to his direction of the Works at Rhymney. His mind had a wide sweep. He was chairman of the Peruvian Bondholders Association and he was not above presiding at the annual Rhymney Eisteddfod. And a corner stone of the London Homeopathic Hospital in Queen's Square and a portrait in the Board Room preserve the memory of his services and his munificence to the hospital over many years.

In the centre of the town was the Lawn, a wooded and park-like enclosure of twenty acres, walled round and protected from intruders. Within it stood three commodious houses, one for the Directors on their infrequent visits, one for the General Manager, and one for the Works' doctor. The populace was permitted to walk in procession through the grounds, once a year, in the form of a bannered host of Sunday Schools. It was the day of the year on which the girls put on their prettiest frocks, so pretty that only our local journalist could do justice to them. This is what he wrote in the summer of 1867 :

" The brilliant state of the weather induced the female population to burst forth from their chrysalis condition during the hibernal and vernal dormancy and appear in all the choice and varied summer hues of the beautiful insect that captivates the eyes of all beholders, and which naturalists are cruel enough to pin in their entymological (sic) cabinets."

The General Manager was the person of first importance in our midst. It was rumoured that he drew a salary of a thousand a year if not more. Below him ranked the departmental Managers, the Furnace, the Bessemer, the Mill Managers, the Engineer, and the Cashier. Several of these had risen from the ranks in one or other of the valleys. At the entrance to the Lawn lived Henry Harris, the Bessemer Manager, in a house which was used to shelter Belgian refugees in the Great War. One of his sons is Professor of Anatomy in the University of Cambridge, and another of Physiology in the University of London. Another manager had four sons, the Price brothers, who in school and chapel have rendered valuable service to Wales.

But in addition to the Works the Company owned a Shop, a Farm, and a Brewery, originally presided over as I have already mentioned by Andrew Buchan. There were branch shops at Twyn Carno, Pontlottyn, Brithdir, and Deri. The manager in the eighties was William Pritchard, an able and upright man of few words and rather forbidding exterior. He hailed from the farm and country inn, called " Cross Oak ", within a mile of Talybont, Breconshire. In 1846, when fourteen, he came to the Lawn Shop and in 1874 he took over the management of the whole concern. He was a member of the Local Board throughout its existence, 1874 to 1894. He was a staunch supporter of agriculture, rode well and was a good judge of horses. Under his sway the shop and brewery horses were always a joy to look upon. My father became his deputy, and—when William Pritchard shot himself in a fit of depression —his successor, in the management of the shop and farm.

The cashier at the shop was John Cartmel, who served the Company from 1850 to 1912. He hailed from Westmorland and made his first journey as a young man to Rhymney by boat to Milford Haven and then by mail coach, taking part of three days for his journey. He was a man of more than average gentleness and refinement and so extremely regular and unruffled in his habits that one could have set one's clock by his movements. I possess one of his notebooks filled with elegant extracts from the poets, chiefly from Byron. He lived to be 94.

A niece of his is Constance Holme, a writer of fiction of sufficient distinction to be included in the *Oxford Classics* in her life-time.

I find it difficult to convey to the reader the central and dominating place occupied by the Old Shop in the life of a small community like that of Rhymney. It was, to begin with, a commodious, solid and stately building, standing in its own grounds, served by its own railway lines, with accommodation for grocery, drapery, ironmongery, furniture, butchery, and baking departments, a slaughter house, stables, warehouse and offices. It was admirably planned and equipped for its purpose as a general store. To a small boy it was a wonderland of romance. Pulleys raised sacks of flour to the top storey ; men in white uniforms stood in a row at the big counter, one weighing tea from great chests on a square of paper fast enough to keep two or three others folding and packing; the cool and spotless butchery with stone floors sprinkled over with fresh sawdust held the carcasses of great beasts hanging from the beams. But best of all was the snug warmth of the stables with the chestnut cobs and ponies, the scent of the leather and the polished harness, and the rattling of the halter chains, the clatter of hooves on the cobbled floor, and the feel of the corn in the bins which I let slip through my fingers like a rosary.

The Rhymney Company Shop was then the only survivor of the numerous truck shops of the early nineteenth century. It possessed no monopoly of the trade of the town. The High Street was interspersed throughout its length with small private shops and the workmen were free to buy in them and clearly did so in considerable numbers. The Company Shop had the advantage of a big store, with every branch under one roof ; its prices were no lower than those of its competitors but its standards of quality were probably higher. My father was for many years the principal buyer in all departments, except drapery. He paid periodic visits to Bristol crossing the Severn by the New Passage, as it was still called. Bristol was the emporium for South Wales, and travellers also came regularly to Rhymney from the great wholesale firms of London, Manchester, and Glasgow.

The shop assistants lived in a large house which formed part of the premises. Their salaries ranged round about £40 —£50 plus board. The carters and stablemen were usually married and lived out.

The relations of the shop and " the Works " were intimate. I may illustrate the connexion from my experience at the Mill Office. John Jones was a mill-hand earning five shillings a day. He was in work on Monday and Tuesday. If he worked a full week he would earn thirty shillings. On Wednesday morning, with my time book before me, I would go through the Order or Advance Book and place twenty-five shillings opposite the name of John Jones keeping the rest " in hand." I would deal similarly with each workman estimating his probable earnings in the week. If for any reason John Jones did not work the full week I would take account of that deficit in the following week or whenever he returned to work. On every page of the Order Book was a column which showed the amount of debt, if any, owed by each workman to the Company Shop and if the amount was substantial it was usual to find a note above the name, e.g., " 1s. per week off " or upwards to as much as 5s. Thus if John Jones owed the Company, say, £10 he would not receive his 25s. but 25s. less two or three shillings a week which went to reduce the debt. On Pay Saturday his accounts, as I have explained earlier, would be made up, any balance due to him paid, and the debt remaining would be brought forward for gradual repayment as before.

The Order Books would be sent from the Mill Office, and the other branch offices, by eleven o'clock on Wednesday mornings to the Pay Office at the Company Shop where lots of women would be waiting. Those who were customers of the shop would put in their account books and would be given a slip of paper on which was written the amount of cash they could draw. With this they would go into the shop itself and buy what they wanted, return to the Pay Office for the cash required to pay for the goods bought, return again to the shop, hand over the money, take away the goods or have them sent to their homes. That was the normal system. Those who were not customers of the shop could take their ' draw ' on Saturdays at the Works Pay Office and spend it where they chose. Other customers would give their ' orders ' to the carters and settle up monthly. In Pay Week when the overdue wages were adjusted there would be very brisk business and the large assembly hall of the grocery department would be full of working women shopping. It was a sociable, talkative crowd, full of rude fun and banter in good times and of pluck and patience in bad. Many would be nursing babies in shawls tightly drawn around their bulbous bosoms and swaying hips. Pregnancy was perpetual with the majority. A mouthful of good teeth was a rare sight and here and there one saw a pock-marked face. The older women could still recall the visitations of cholera in 1849, in 1854, and in 1866, when thirty-two persons died within a fortnight. There were the frugal who feared to get into debt and the debauched who never expected to get out of debt. Babies, weddings, funerals, strikes and lock-outs were the original sources of debt, and drink was

THE COMPANY SHOP TO-DAY

an unfailing fountain. " Hen Gownt " (old account) was the euphemism for long-standing debt and some families stood in the books owing eighty or a hundred pounds.

Such was the Truck System in its last surviving citadel. Away back in 1831 an Anti-Truck Act had been passed which repealed centuries of previous legislation. It announced in its preamble that it was necessary to prohibit the payment in certain trades of wages in goods or otherwise than in the current coin of the realm. But the iron-masters circumvented the Act and there was no effective inspection. Among the causes adduced to explain the rise of Chartism a few years later was the prevalence of Truck. Shops continued to be run directly or indirectly by the Companies at Dowlais, Ebbw Vale, Blaen-avon and Blaina.

In 1852 an interesting case was brought against the Rhymney Iron Company. A collier had been in the employ of the Company from January, 1850, to November, 1851. He had earned £64 15s. 9d., and had received £24 16s. 6d. in cash after the usual deductions for the doctor's fund. He contended that the payment to him of the remaining £39 19s. 3d., being a payment in goods and not in cash was void under the 1831 Act (1 & 2 William IV C37). In the course of the trial it was proved that of the workmen in the employ of the Company during 1850-51, 437 did not deal at the shop ; that 409 dealt partially at the shop ; and that about 1,300 workmen were regular customers.

The Judge divided the sum claimed into two parts deter-mined by the occurrence of a certain conversation. From January, 1850, to January, 1851, when £22 16s. 10d. had been spent in goods there was no evidence of any influence to induce plaintiff to deal at the shop, and he gave judgement for the

Company in that amount. But with regard to £17 2s. 5d. he gave judgment for the plaintiff considering that plaintiff did deal at the shop under some degree of constraint. An overman in a conversation with the collier had produced a list of names from the cost clerk " to remember the names that did not deal at the shop." That proved fatal despite the effort of the Company to disavow responsibility for the overman's action. The court did not disapprove of the payment of wages " in the current coin of the realm " at the shop Pay Office and the practice continued for nearly forty years before another conviction was obtained which finally ended the system.

Meanwhile the Government held an enquiry in 1871 and the Commissioners in reviewing the evidence declared that the Rhymney shop was well conducted and it was quite possible to keep clear of it. Two thirds of the workmen did so. There were 105 shops in the village and of 71 of these the Company were the ground landlords and could prevent any of these shops being let. The " draws " amounted to 66 per cent. of the earnings. The total wages earned at the central Rhymney works in 1869 was £200,137. Of this £132,310 was paid before pay day in the shape either of draws or advances. £62,723 of the advances were taken to the shop. By far the largest custom was done with the advance men on the tacit understanding that their " subs." were to be expended on shop goods. This class of workmen was the poorest and most improvident. " The real pressure lies not in the cash advance clerk or the shop manager's conduct, but in the system of lengthened pays and draws, which is so adjusted as to render it far more convenient for the needy workman to betake himself to the shop and to accept all its terms." For the Company it was argued that when the pays were short the loss of time from drinking

" D.B." ON SAUCY BOY

at the Pay made it difficult to keep the works going from want of coal.

At last, in May, 1885, primed by a group of local shop-keepers, the Solicitor to the Treasury took proceedings at a special petty session held at Tredegar. Distinguished counsel were engaged, Danckwerts for the Crown and Jelf for the Company. The court was packed like a herring barrel. The magistrates decided that there was a Truck Shop at Rhymney and imposed penalties of 40s. in the first case, and 5s. in the second. The third case lasted several hours and the Bench by a majority imposed a fine of 40s. The fines were inflicted without costs. Thus ended the old regime founded by Andrew Buchan, and from this time forward the shop continued to do business without the intervention of a Pay Office on the premises.

Debt and dishonesty were the bugbears of my father's life and indolence he could not abide. He had brought with him from his home in the country great physical strength, energy and self-reliance. He had not a lazy bone in his body. When a boy of thirteen he had been sent from Llangeitho to Aberaeron in sole charge of a waggon and a pair of horses, with £70 in a bag under a sack in the corner of the cart to pay travellers and order goods. At that time goods came to Aberaeron by boat from England. As a young man in Rhymney he could carry two sacks of flour on his back and he learnt to pack tea and sugar as fast as the fastest. He could swing a scythe, skin a sheep, fell an ox with one blow, sit a horse and jump a fence. He often acted as judge of dairy produce at Agricultural Shows. This ability to do any other man's job throughout the shop and to do it well brought him to the top of the business. With education he would have gone much further. He rarely spoke of himself. He had no politics.

He deplored children's loss of respect for their elders, which he attributed to Board Schools. He was infinitely kind to his own children in material ways, and slaved for them, but he could not be a companion to them. Nature gave him a big heart, and grace filled it with generosity. He was given neither to scandal nor intrigue. He had no trace of cupidity or meanness. He let me go my way, let me save my wages in order to go to college, found all the money he could to help me along at Aberystwyth and Glasgow, and never once questioned my use of it. This unselfish and generous outlook he shared with our mother who was always sending beef-tea or chicken-broth or sago to the sick. Preachers especially were made welcome and were given of our very best. What Giraldus said of the Welsh was true of our home : " They consider liberality and hospitality amongst the first virtues." Supper on Sunday nights was a communal feast when we reacted from the spiritual exercises of the day around a generous table. Perhaps, as Saintsbury would put it, we thought too highly of mint sauce, but the preacher if he were a man at all and worth his salt would regale us with a dessert of good stories.

My father had a simple faith in the Bible and believed in its verbal inspiration. He wrote verses from it in pocket-books and on scraps of packing paper and committed them to memory at odd moments. They acted as a charm. He was occasionally called upon to value the furniture and assets of public houses belonging to the Brewery when they changed tenants. In the course of these duties he would come across neglected Family Bibles which he bought in and brought home so that they might no longer suffer indignity.

He was, like many another, less fitted for the top than for second place. He had a quick temper, far too quick to allow him, like Darius Clayhanger, to look forward to it as some men look forward to brandy. Though he never got nearer to damning than "Dank it all," when roused his language could be violent and his charges grossly unfair and exaggerated. If I were near I could protect his victims and check his rage, but he did not surrender easily and he was not given to apologise. His sharp and experienced eye dared in all directions "all over the shop," and the sight of slovenly or stupid work made him blaze. "His heart was much better than his tongue" wrote one of his assistants at his death in 1919. He prided himself on his speed and our mother fed the illusion. He claimed that he could change faster for a funeral than any assistant, but then my mother laid his clothes and elastic-sided boots ready for him when he rushed in. Once, when he got tangled and fretted with studs and a refractory collar, he ripped the shirt from top to bottom, stamped on it, and called for another, which his patient wife produced without a murmur.

The Company Shop was closed in 1911 and my father moved to Cardiff where he made new friends in the local Welsh Methodist Chapel. At home he found comfort in reading the denominational periodicals and the Bible and in copying out aphorisms from William Penn's *Fruits of Solitude* which I had left lying about. He died during the railway strike of 1919 and almost his last words were a request that the charwoman should be given a good meal before she left the house. As the funeral approached the grave on the hillside above Rhymney I was handed a telegram. It was from Sir Maurice Hankey summoning me to take the Minutes of an urgent and unexpected meeting of the Cabinet. That would have pleased my father. I motored back to London through the night.

.    .    .    .    .    .    .    .    .

Five-and-twenty years after the closing of the Company Shop it was visited by the King of England. In the meantime it had fallen into ruins but latterly a small part of it had been tidied up and turned to the purposes of a club for unemployed miners, where they cobbled shoes, did a bit of carpentry, smoked and gossiped through weeks and months of enforced idleness. On an afternoon in November, 1936, Edward the Eighth arrived at the Shop with his Ministers and staff. Nowhere was he more popular than in South Wales ; nothing was known of his impending fate. He was welcomed with wild enthusiasm. He appeared very tired but when he got inside the building and found only unemployed men and women and these in small groups in various rooms, he became very cheerful, chatted freely and laughed and joked. The British Legion paraded rather pathetically before His Majesty. The miners sang to him *Y Deryn Pur* and *Cwm Rhondda*. Characteristically he asked about my associations with the old Shop. He left the building for the railway station close by, where he rejoined his train for the return to London. This was his last public appearance until the final broadcast. In less than a month from his visit to Rhymney he had ceased to be King of England.

THE WORKS TO-DAY

# CHAPTER X

## CHAPEL : (i) TEACHERS

*The terms may change ; the truth endures. We can feel that we are greater than we know ; we cannot by any trick of substitution know ourselves greater than we are. The meanings grow ; the mind is purified ; experience gathers mass and momentum ; crypt, nave and vaulting stand solid, sensitive and true ; till, at last, among many spires, the loftiest rises to its exactly-calculated height, and is crowned with the prepared stone which completes the edifice.*

Times Literary Supplement *on* Dante's *Divine Comedy.*

I HAVE traced the course of my education in schools, in streets and in offices but I have said little or nothing of the education which proceeded from my association with a chapel. There was a large choice : Ebenezer, Zion, Penuel, Tabernacle, Goshen, Brynhyfryd, Moriah, Jerusalem. This list omits the Anglican and Roman Catholic churches and the English nonconformist churches. We had besides, a small room-full of Latter Day Saints, and two or three who dabbled in Spiritualism and went to secret seances. A mesmerist who came amongst us with his black art was publicly mobbed. My choice in fact was pre-determined by my Calvinistic ancestry. My great-grandfather, grandfather, his brother, and my own father were deacons of the Welsh Calvinistic Methodist or Presbyterian Church.

Christianity in Calvin's view was opposed to all disorder and Calvinism became not only a coherent structure of thought but also a highly organised system of church government;

an organism in which the churches were held together, and all the members, deacons and ministers were placed in order and kept in order by a hierarchy of courts from the single congregation, through the district meeting, the monthly meeting, the quarterly meeting up to the General Assembly. The result was that if you were brought up, as I was, within this " Connexion " or " Body " you lived in an *imperium in imperio*, a state within a state. I felt and knew myself to be a Methodist much more actively and intensely than I felt myself to be a Welshman. I knew nothing of Welsh history in my formative years. O. M. Edwards was to come later with his intriguing books and magazines, and our first Cymru Fydd society in Rhymney was not founded until 1895. Calvinism, and still more the church of the Reformation, was an organisation not bounded by Cardiff and Holyhead. Its spiritual impulse had spread over Europe and America, animating and shaping the lives of puritans, republicans, and democrats. Outside the realm of religion Wales had no rich massive historical tradition, widespread and familiar, capable of dominating the mind of youth brought up in a border bilingual village. I have been much more shaped by the Wales of the Preachers than by the Wales of the Princes or the Wales of the Politicians. The first reformers wrought the great change in Wales by moving the feelings of the congregation rather than by instructing their minds. But in course of time this led to a valuable system of theological education for children and adults, through colleges, through the pulpit, through Sunday Schools, and through periodical literature. I was to profit by this fusion of feeling and intellect.

My theological education began as a very young child when, because it was too wet or for some other reason, I was

not taken to chapel on Sunday evenings and was left in charge
of the servant, Mary Ann Perry. She was just able to read
and the book we studied together was the *Peep of Day*. She
had a tender heart and as we spelt it out together the tears would
trickle down her cheeks. It was from these pages that I got
my first ideas of the moral foundations of the universe, was
handed the first key with which to unlock the mysteries of the
world in which I found myself. These little books served
the purpose of an index or filing system; a framework of iron
dogma, if you like, providing an orderly arrangement of the
world and its history for the young mind, under two main
categories, Good and Evil. The simplicity of the language
masked the sublimity of the subject. The author, Farell Lee
Bevan, has told us that she aimed at the superlative degree
of littleness. By this means she found her way into the simple
minds of children and lowly folk as few have done before or
since. The edition I have before me is dated 1888 and
marked Seven hundred and Fifty-ninth Thousand. That
was fifty years ago. It has been translated into about forty
languages.

It is sad to learn that the author's married life was unhappy.
Dr. Edwyn Bevan has told us that his aunt took six or seven
poor orphans to live with her on the East coast and that while
she could show charming solicitude for her proteges she could
also be an autocratic lawgiver. Her donkey was driven blind-
fold into the sea, still harnessed to the cart, because sea-bathing
was good for it.

The lamb was also subjected to sea-bathing; the
problem of drying its soaked fleece my aunt solved with
characteristic ingenuity: she had it left buried for a time
in the sand, with only its nose protruding. She herself

was a regular bather : the orphans were made to stand
in a circle, holding up towels, with their backs inwards
while she solemnly undressed in the middle.

(*Times*, 27th June, 1933).

Dr. Johnson says he remembers when he first heard of
heaven and hell. So do I. It was in the pages of the *Peep
of Day* and the *Mother's Gift*. The former had short chapters
followed by simple poems ; the latter was a Welsh catechism.
It was picture-thinking, called by scholars ' apocalyptic ' and
familiar to us especially in the Book of Revelations, in Dante,
Milton, and Bunyan. Here is an example from the *Peep of Day* :

### ON THE WICKED ANGELS

Heaven and Hell were arranged above and below and
the earth was placed between—tier upon tier—God in
supreme splendour on the summit of a throne, surrounded
by hosts of angels in a kingdom of light everlasting, and
down below in the kindgom of darkness, Satan, surrounded
by hosts of demons, ruling the tortured and  tormented
lost souls through eternity.

The sermons of the great Welsh preachers are full of picture-
thinking and it is an incomparable medium for reaching the
multitude. Mr. Lloyd George has used this gift and anyone
who has analysed a popular speech by him has found it to be
a series of pictures and metaphors. Pulpit imagery varied
in artistic quality. Pedrog quotes a preacher who declared
that the whale went as near the shore as possible, then put out
his tongue like a plank to the beach so that Jonah could walk
along it comfortably. My grandfather liked to quote a verse
from the *Spiritual Railway* which he had heard the Rev. Evan
Harris, Merthyr, use :

> Come now, poor sinner, now's the time
> In any station on the line ;
> If you'll repent and turn from sin
> The train will stop and take you in.

The next instruments of my theological education were the Sunday School and the Children's Meeting. In the former my teacher was John Davies, a minor poet, known in Wales as Ossian Gwent, for he published two volumes of verse. He was a patternmaker, the basis of which is a knowledge of carpentry. He was thus one of the trained craftsmen, careful, patient and exact, of whom at that time we had many—men who had served a seven years' apprenticeship to a trade and who prided themselves on their skill, and delighted in making articles for their homes in wood or metal. The carpenters made writing cabinets, money-boxes, rulers, paper knives ; the blacksmiths and fitters made fire-irons, screens, tuning forks, railway carriage keys, triangles. The presence in our little community of a body of men with aesthetic instincts trained in practical ways had much to do with the high standard of cleanliness, order and neatness in a large number of working-class homes. Well-made pieces of domestic furniture were still abundant.

Ossian Gwent was a gentle and refined soul. He wrote lovingly of birds and flowers, says his translator truly, but theology would sometimes break in, as in this verse to the Bible :

> 'Tis like some fair sea shell—
> Bend down thine ear
> And thou shalt hear
> The river on the golden strand
> And sound of harps in that fair land
> Or wails of souls in hell.

When we put questions which were beyond him he would postpone answering them to the following Sunday and sometimes he would lend me a book which would help me out. We had puzzled him with conundrums about the crowing of the cock in the gospel story. He gave me the *Land and the Book* by a Dr. Thomson, who had been for thirty years a missionary in Syria and Palestine. It described a journey from Lebanon to Jerusalem in an easy conversational narrative and there were many illustrations of trees and birds and costumes and customs of the Holy Land. He settled the question as follows :

> Is not the cock-crowing a very indefinite division of time ? I have noticed throughout our wanderings that they seem to crow all night long—it is, however, while the dawn is struggling into day that the whole band of chanticleers blow their shrill clarions with the greatest energy and emulation. It seems to be an objection to the sign given to Peter, that a thousand cocks in Jerusalem might crow at any hour. For him, however, it was sufficient that in the house of Caiaphas there was but one which gave forth its significant note in immediate response to his cruel and cowardly denial of his Lord and it answered the purpose intended perfectly.

With this book and others like it I got to be very familiar with the geography and topography of Palestine, more intimately familiar indeed than with that of England and Wales at this period. That was true of generations of Welsh boys and I think it was this preparation which predisposed Mr. Lloyd George to support Dr. Weizmann and the Balfour Declaration in favour of Zionism in 1917. Anyway Hazlitt was right. " It is delightful . . . to travel out of one's self into the Chaldee,

Hebrew and Egyptian characters ; to have the palm trees waving mystically in the margin of the page, and the camels moving slowly on in the distance of three thousand years."

In the Children's Meeting the method was that of the catechism. It is the mark of a civilized man, says Ezra Pound, that he gives serious answers to serious questions. That is what we did. Our conductor was a man with a shake and shiver in his voice and his tremulous tearful style had an immense effect on the children, and we answered together in an ever swelling chorus as follows, but of course in Welsh :

Can God do whatever He pleases ?

Yes, ' for with God all things are possible.'

Is God just ?

Yes, 'the Lord is righteous in all His ways, and holy in all His works.'

How many kind of children are there ?

Two kinds.

Which are the two kinds ?

Good children, and bad children. ' In this the children of God are manifest, and the children of the Devil.'

The minute study of texts, which assumed the theory of verbal inspiration, was carried to extreme lengths of speculative ingenuity and often degenerated into absurdity. Threshing straw, Sir Henry Jones used to call it. I have heard it argued that the cleverness of the Jews originated in the microscopic study of the Talmud and it may be that the subtlety with which the Welsh are credited (or debited) by the English is traceable to similar excessive logical analysis of the letter of Scripture. The art of catechising the adult members of the congregations, gathered together from a group of Sunday Schools to be examined on some portion of Scripture or specific doctrine, was sometimes conducted with great skill. It has been inimitably described by Professor W. J. Gruffydd in his *Hen Atgofion*. Hitler uses it in a simplified form adapted to evoke tremendous mass emotion at the annual rally of the Nazi Party at Nuremberg.

John Donne summed up characteristically this habit of detaching single sentences : " Sentences in scripture, like hairs in horsetails, concur in one root of beauty and strength ; but being plucked out one by one, serve only for springs and snares." This may be true of adults, but short extracts were as much as the child's memory could carry.   Single verses, drawn freely from all parts of the Bible, and printed on cards with coloured borders were given to us at each attendance, and a larger card in return for a number of them, and then a certificate for framing as a final reward.   The framing of biblical texts and proverbs prescribing virtue, and admonitions to redeem the time, for there were but sixty minutes in the hour, was common.   And I recall a Christian calendar published in Machynlleth in the sixties with an extract for each day from the writings of 365 theologians, English and Welsh.   It had some very apocalyptic entries.   For example :

Dec. 11. It will be a great thing to have below and above thee, without and within thee, a boiling fire—without hope of salvation, one everlasting Waterloo.

There was no limit to the subjects to which the method of question and answer could be applied for  the instruction of the young and the Bible itself provided the only limit to the supply of supporting texts.   These texts, drawn from Genesis to Revelation, all equal in value as evidence, could be marshalled by the children themselves and in this way a valuable foundation was laid for a wide knowledge of the scriptures.   Here, for example, are questions and answers freely translated from a catechism on Church Praise, published at Bala in 1810, the verses for which were collected by the young people of Capel Curig.

*Q.* Is it seemly that the praise of God in church should be in groups, such as Bass, Tenor and Treble ?

*A.* It is certainly not a sin for it was so arranged under the old dispensation, especially in the time of David, Solomon, Jehosaphat, Hezechiah, Ezra and Nehemiah, the men used by God to establish his cause.

The proof adduced is from Psalm 150 where the Lord is praised with psaltery and harp ; with timbrel and dance ; with stringed instruments and organs.

*Q.* Do you think there will be musical instruments in the evangelical church in the Great Revival as under the old dispensation ?

*A.* No, we do not. Musical instruments foreshadowed the rejoicing of the evangelical church and were not a rule to be followed. They will not be necessary in the days to come for the singers of the church will be perfect and their music will embrace all melody and harmony whatsoever.

Some ingenuity had to be exercised in establishing this thesis and the result is not very convincing. The proof was found in Zechariah xii, 8, and in Isaiah xxx, 26 :

The light of the moon shall be as the light of the sun, and the light of the sun shall be sevenfold, as the light of seven days, in the day that the Lord bindeth up the breach of his people, and healeth the stroke of their wound.

The minute study of the Scriptures was fostered by a system of graded Sunday School examinations and the publication annually of commentaries by divines belonging to the denomination. I sat the first of these, open to the county, in 1884, and came out seventh out of sixty-seven with my name printed in the *Amseroedd (Times)*, an unforgettable milestone.    I kept the cutting for years.    I finished up in 1890 by being bracketed first for the Gold Medal, open to all members of the denomination, an achievement which gave my father and mother more pleasure than anything else I ever did.    Between these two dates I had been increasingly fascinated by the study of theology and my interest in double-entry book-keeping, digesting returns, indexing, docketing and the other subjects of the Civil Service syllabus suffered a decline, which fortunately coincided with the postponement of the examination for Lower Division Clerkships.    I read regularly the monthly *Drysorfa (Treasury)*, printed from fresh clean type on good paper by the R. E. Jones Brothers, Conway.    I was predisposed by 'the feel' of this magazine to read it.

A third instrument of popular education in our village was the Penny Reading, usually held as a counter attraction to the public houses on Saturday nights.    Prizes were given for reading prose passages from which all punctuation marks had been omitted, for singing sol-fa passages—with frequent changes of key—at sight, for recitations, for solo singing, and for essays and impromptu speeches.    Some of these were prolific of merriment, especially the first and second.    The rate at which the sol-faists had sometimes to negotiate their doh-ray-mes forced them to twist their mouths into fantastic shapes and the solemn airs of the tragic reciters were hardly less mirth-provoking.    Joseph Davies, endowed by nature with high cheek bones and a pallid and dark countenance, would recite *Y Ddaeargryn* (The Earthquake) or *Ymson y Llofrudd*

(The Murderer's Soliloquy) " by request." He would sit on the vestry platform, on a space cleared for action, in the imaginary prison, slowly awaking from a dream, and with eyes half-open would presently discern a spot of blood remaining on the hand which had done the deed. " Blood ? " he would breathe incredulously with shocked self-surprise but quietly. " No, not blood," he would reply to himself in a loud whisper. " No, not blood," he repeated with hesitation. Then with the full horror of the deed breaking upon him he would suddenly leap up and shout till the rafters rang : " Ie, gwaed." (Yes blood), and all the youngsters in the front seats would laugh and ruin the effect. And there was a Twyncarno tailor who recited in Welsh with an Oxford accent, so to say. His favourite effort was *Y Côr Mawr* (pronounced Mewr) (The Big Choir). This was a detailed description, down to the whistle of the steam-engine, of the visit of Caradog's choir from South Wales in 1873 to compete at the Crystal Palace, and its triumphant return with the prize. The adjudicators were Sir Julius Benedict, Sir John Goss and Sir Joseph Barnby, and the six set pieces : *The many rend the skies* (Handel), *I wrestle and pray* (Bach), *Dies Irae* (Cherubini), *Hallelujah to the Father* (Beethoven), *See what love hath the Father*, and *Come with Torches* (Mendelssohn).

Memory was widely cultivated by this practice of public recitation and by learning chapters of the Bible which would sometimes be said aloud by a member of the congregation instead of being read by the minister. Once as a *tour de force* Psalm 119 was declaimed in this way. When Bardd Coch (Red Bard) returned from the United States to visit his home in Rhymney he was welcomed in a public meeting and he entertained the audience for two hours reciting poetry from memory. But we were even more famed for our songsters. One of our own Brynhyfryd members was *The Nightingale of Monmouthshire* and we had another in the village, *The Nightingale of the Mill Brook*. And there was plain John Thomas who was more than once victorious in the solo at the National Eisteddfod. And I must not omit Benjie Bach. He was a small thin wisp of a man, with jet black hair, oiled and curled. He stood erect with his head thrown back and slightly to one side, his eyes sparkling like diamonds, as he sang divinely the *Death of Nelson*, beating time with his knock knees. In the bar of a local public house the landlord wished to close and threatened to turn out Benjie Bach. " You might as well try to shift Snowdon ", said the little man, made brave by beer. These were all tenors. We also had our quota of soprano, contralto, and bass soloists who could stand and sing unabashed in the face of the sun and the eye of light. D. B. Evans was a bass whose voice spanned two octaves. Popular songs were *Maid of Athens Ere We Part, Larboard Watch, The White Squall*, the duet from Dr. Joseph Parry's *Blodwen, Tell Me Gentle Stranger*, and *In the Dusk of the Twilight*. Another favourite duet was *Flow gently, Deva*, the opening words of which went somewhat as follows :

> Flow gently, Deva,
> On thy mossy banks
> The valiant Tudor sleeps.
> Sweet be his dreams
> And when he wakes
> O ! may he wake to peace.

Alas ! he did not. The dashing sound of arms roused the gallant Tudor from his slumbers, but whether he led us to death or victory I have forgotten. There was a tradition current that one of our soloists, William Williams, the painter,

had such a powerful voice that once when singing in a local
hall the glass of the windows broke. And in 1860 eight of
these musical giants went to Abergavenny Eisteddfod to sing
*The Horse and its Rider*, a piece suitable for a choir of 200. They
won the prize. I do not remember *Penillion* (stanzas) being sung
to the harp by any native of the town, though I have often heard
them since, and was reminded of them when reading of a new
kind of song, called *chastushka*, in vogue among the factory
workers of Soviet Russia. It is described as a short tune in
duple time, set for dancing, to which singers easily improvise
verses, often of a very humorous kind. The name comes
from a word meaning " close together " or " frequent." There's
no limit to the number of verses, so the tune repeats frequently,
and since it is a short quick tune, the accented beats occur with
frequent regularity.

But the musical efforts of individual soloists were dwarfed
by the achievements of the Rhymney choirs. There were,
sometimes simultaneously, three of these : the large mixed
choir, the male voice choir, and the ladies choir. Each of them
won at the National Eisteddfod, the larger choir five times,
three times in succession. In 1911 it was invited to represent
Wales at the Empire Festival at the Crystal Palace. Its conductor was a self-taught musician and a school attendance
officer. The male voice conductor was a miner and the ladies
choir was led by a young woman who ran a bakehouse. The
rank and file produced their own leaders and obeyed them.
They had little experience of the world outside the village.
One of them, some years later, sailing from Liverpool to the
States mistook the tender for the liner. The last rehearsal
before the choir set out on its journey next morning to the
contest at the National Eisteddfod was always a thrilling exper-

ience, often more musically impressive than the final rendering in the pavilion, where the rivalry and the repetition of the test pieces introduced disturbing elements.   At home, in one of the larger chapels, the men in black, the women in white, row upon row rising to the rafters of the gallery, every eye riveted on the conductor, the men erect, the women more eager, bending slightly forward, all voices blending perfectly, all faces rapt in ecstacy, the singers were wafted away to a heaven of pure delight far far away from furnaces and coalpits.

This wide diffusion of choral singing and the frequent rehearsals throughout the winter provided a delightful recreation for many hundreds of men and women despite the rivalries and jealousies between choir and choir which marred the harmony.   Every member was not only a performer but a musical critic.   There can have been few homes in which snatches from the great oratorios and the set test pieces were not familiar.   Handel, Haydn, Mendelssohn, and Joseph Parry, once a Dowlais puddler, were the popular composers.   Bach and Beethoven were for the majority still in the future waiting to be introduced by Sir Walford Davies.   From the male voice party we were always hearing the *Destruction of Gaza*, *Martyrs of the Arena*, *Italian Salad*, *Tyrol*, and *War Horse*.   This last by David Jenkins of Aberystwyth was based on a famous passage in the Book of Job where the war horse " smelleth the battle afar off."   He was also the composer of *David and Saul*, which the Rhymney choir, led by Tom Price, sang at the Merthyr National Eisteddford in 1881.   Ben Davies and James Savage were the soloists and I, a boy of eleven, sold programmes to the 3,000 present.

More closely associated with the chapels were the Singing Festivals of the various denominations where a day was given up to hymn and anthem singing under the baton of some well known professional conductor from outside, who in addition to being a musician had usually to belong to the denomination which was holding the festival. There was hardly a region, sacred or secular, into which sectarianism did not penetrate.

One other form of democratic education I may mention at this point were the friendly societies : Foresters, Oddfellows, Buffaloes, Ivorites, Shepherds, Philanthropics, Ancient Britons, Railway Servants. There were between thirty and forty Courts, Lodges, or Branches and four or five Money Clubs, all of which met in the public houses. The superior artisans subscribed by post to the Hearts of Oak Society in London ; managers and the chief shopkeepers met in a Freemasons Lodge. There were also agents of the many collecting insurance societies : the Prudential, Pearl, Britannic, Refuge, Rational, Royal London, Royal Liver, Bristol and West of England, London, Edinburgh, and Glasgow—all had local representatives. But the friendly societies had not only local officers, but regular meetings, an elaborate ritual and a degree of mystery surrounding them. I never got nearer penetrating their privacy than when I went to pay my father's weekly dues to the Oddfellows at the Castle Hotel and was offered and refused a tot of beer through a small sliding aperture or guichet. I was myself a member of a children's lodge of the Rechabites. We too had our official positions and titles, and very wonderful they were. I stood and called the meeting to order with a tap of a mallet, like the President of a World Conference. We also had splendid regalia and banners. Napoleon said you could manage men if you gave them toys and decorations to play with. Certainly Thomas Williams managed us easily in the vestry of Tabernacle Chapel and with permanent results, for I have never quite rid myself of a prejudice against alcohol or ceased to feel secretly censorious when seeing others consuming it, despite strenuous efforts to be broad-minded. The ruin of gifted and charming natures of both sexes which I witnessed in my youth took all the joy out of alcohol for me for the rest of my life. No doubt I should have been more shocked by other vices.

It was a community which seized on any pretext for getting together. Sunday School treat, church conversazione, male voice party convivial meeting, clothing or money club tea and coffee supper, colliery officials dinner, bachelors banquet, shop assistants picnic, brewery staff sea trip, postmen and fire brigade excursion, variegated the annual calendar of events. And presentations from a grateful public to some faithful servant were frequent. A portrait in oils by William Harris, Merthyr, was the normal expression of our gratitude.

> If a likeness you are seeking
> For yourself, or one for treating,
> That shall be at once most speaking—
>     To Harris go.

The rate collector for over thirty years reported that during all that time there was not a penny of the rates owing to the District Council. We gave him a casket of cutlery from Walker and Hall, Sheffield. An overman was promoted to be manager of a neighbouring colliery, so we gave him an illuminated address, executed by the *Western Mail,* Cardiff. It read like this :

> We consider it no degradation to mention a fact which you are not ashamed to acknowledge, that you have been a hard working man. The fact that we are going to lose your services causes pangs of untold grief to pierce our hearts, but your appointment as head-manager causes

us untold joy. We now commend you to the care of Almighty God, ' for the pillars of the earth are the Lord's, and He hath set the world upon them, and His eyes run to and fro through the whole earth.'

Once a silver cup was to have been presented to a local engineer on his becoming an Associate of the Institute of Civil Engineers, but he died before receiving it. On it had been cut these lines :

To him whom Science proud her son must deem,
Rhymney awards this token of esteem ;
Till life's bright star beyond its verge doth sink
From this to Rhymney shall her favourite drink.


## (ii) DEACONS

*Anthony, thou art not so perfect as a cobbler that dwelleth in Alexandria.*

LIVES OF THE SAINTS.

CALVINISM is an impressive example of the permeating power of ideas in the realm of religion and politics. It set out to confront the might of Rome in the first quarter of the sixteenth century from a small Swiss town of 13,000 inhabitants. Geneva was then not much larger than the Welsh village I have been describing but it was sternly ruled by a man whom Hooker described as incomparably " the wisest man that ever the French Church did enjoy since the hour it enjoyed him."

John Calvin was not twenty-seven when he published the *Institutes of the Christian Religion,* a work which was to influence for centuries the mind and conduct of multitudes in many lands. Comte omitted Calvin from his calendar of great men whereupon Lord Morley observed that to do so was to read the history of Western evolution with one eye shut. About the same time Dr. Dale of Birmingham declared that had Ireland only been Calvinistic we should have had no Irish problem. It is strange that Disraeli in the famous passage on genius and youth in *Coningsby* should mention as working with young brains Luther, Loyola, Wesley and Pascal and should omit Calvin. Today it is usual to bracket Calvin and Marx together not only because each had a doctrine of predestination but because of their world-wide influence. Calvinism saved Europe, Mark Pattison declared. It remains to be seen what Marxism will do. Wales was formally joined to England in 1536, the year in which Calvin published the *Institutes*. It took two centuries from that date for the influence of the *Institutes* to spread effectively in the Principality. There is much in the religious life of Wales in the nineteenth century to remind the student of seventeenth century England. In the eighteenth century Wales took in the main the Calvinistic road rather than the Arminian, following George Whitfield rather than John Wesley. A determining factor in this development was the Calvinistic doctrine of the catechisms used in the circulating schools promoted by Griffith Jones of Llanddowror, and the influence of Griffith Jones on a great preacher, Daniel Rowlands, and on a great educator, Thomas Charles of Bala. In course of time each doctrine modified the other. Speaking to an assembly of Wesleyans at Aberystwyth in 1891, Principal Thomas Charles Edwards summed up the position : "You did not found Welsh Methodism. You did not originate our spiritual societies. You have softened the asperity of our Calvinism. You have made it more human, more genial, and today we are not ashamed of it."

It is Calvin's distinction to have found a place for laymen in the government of the Church. He laid it down that with pastors and teachers were to be joined certain pious, grave, and holy men as a senate in each church and that the election of these officers was to be with the people. This was in complete contrast with the practice of the Roman Church in the pre-reformation world and was to have far reaching importance for political democracy. It not only delivered men from subjection to priests and parsons but it stood them on their feet erect in the presence of their political and economic rulers. The reformist doctrines of the value of the individual soul and the right of personal access of each man to God combined with the layman's right to an effective share in the Government of the Church endowed the commonest man with dignity and helped to counter the paralysis and resignation inherent in Calvin's absolutist and fatalist theories. It held the seed of Liberalism and wherever the seed fell freedom sprouted.

The population of Rhymney was divided into three classes : those who went to the State or Anglican Church, those who went to the Nonconformist Chapels, and those who went nowhere but remained outside in "the World." Church discipline was still operative in my youth but it was nothing like as severe as in the Geneva of Calvin. He admitted to Farel that it was not possible to refuse men all amusements. Cards had been forbidden because they led men to trust to luck instead of to labour. Calvin wrote in the *Institutes* that he was not so superstitious as to object to all "visible representations" but he would limit the range of subjects to be painted or sculptured. With later Calvinists as with Quakers this took the form of objecting to being photographed as savouring of pride and worldliness and though my grandfather was photographed under protest he used to quote to me "thou shalt not make unto thyself any graven image" as decisive. And throughout his life he refused to take out an insurance policy because to so do would show a lack of faith in Providence. It was Prince Hohenlohe who defined a Calvinist as a man who never had a good glass of wine, never kissed a pretty girl, and never had a well fitting pair of trousers. In addition to these deprivations dancing was also tabooed in Wales though not universally in Scotland. Step-dancing with clappers, for drinks, was confined in Rhymney to the public houses.

The one subject on which the churches in Rhymney gave forth an uncertain sound was that of total abstinence. The existence of the Brewery in our midst had something to do with this hesitation. Many church members were employed there. The temperance movement was only some thirty or forty years old in 1870. My great-grandfather brewed some sort of beer on his own premises and the preachers staying with him partook of it. Neither my grandfather nor my father were abstainers though my father was always extremely temperate, compromising on cider, and when the Church ruled that deacons should totally abstain he conformed. There were as many public house as chapels in the village, all belonging to the Company, and as well-conducted, I believe, as any to be found in the valleys. Excessive drinking was the most obvious cause of misery in our midst. Its victims were to be found in all classes of the little community. Saturday nights, especially Pay Saturday nights, when there was a lot of money about, were apt to be disfigured by an orgy of drunkenness and brutal exhibitions of fighting. As a timekeeper I was daily confronted with proof of these excesses in the form of absenteeism and broken time. The Company could console itself with the reflection that what they lost on the swings as employers they gained on the roundabouts as brewers.

The reader must bear in mind that in the previous thirty years the village had rapidly expanded by the influx of new-comers with diverse standards and traditions. There was something akin to colonisation in the settlement of these indus-trial valleys. Colonists opened up the New World with a crucifix in one hand and a sword in the other. The South Wales pioneers brought Breweries along with the Bible. *Video non posse negari omnia oblectamenta*—if I may requote Calvin's admission to Farel.

Church discipline had been relaxed from its former severity by my time, but there still prevailed an effective public opinion and definite standards. To fall below these shocked the *âme rigide de la province*. Church membership meant an open and public affirmation of a desire to attempt to respond to the tremendous demands which Christianity makes upon its adher-ents. That these demands were found excessive by many was evidenced by the existence not only of Laodiceans within the fold, but of a class known as *gwrandawyr* or listeners, who frequented the church services with the discriminating exception of the Communion service, and sometimes sat apart from the congregation in the gallery. They might attend the Prayer Meeting on Monday evening but not the Church Meeting on Thursday. In these two meetings men and women sat apart in the vestry in two distinct groups.

Calvin's injunction about the place of laymen determined, in the course of the centuries, that Brynhyfryd Chapel in the eighteen-seventies should be ruled by a senate or diaconate consisting of a green-grocer, a draper, a cobbler, and a store-keeper. The storekeeper was my grandfather and he was acknowledged spontaneously as the chief deacon, in virtue neither of wealth nor position, for he had neither, but because he transcended his colleagues as a Christian.  He was a gentleman born and a Christian by adoption.  Doubtless there have been churches where deacons were elected for other reasons than the possession of Christian virtues above their brethren.  There have been good men " in the worst sense of the term." These have been sufficiently mocked and ridiculed by our postwar dramatists.  I have read of an American work entitled *An Impartial History of the Civil War* : *From the Southern Point of View*.  That is the sort of impartiality I feel as a grandson of Enoch Jones.

I have already said something of my grandfather's early education and his employment first as a miner and then for the rest of his life as the chief dispenser of stores—picks, shovels, files, nails, leather belting, explosives, whatever short of complete engines and machines was required to supply the multifarious needs of an organisation engaged in getting coal and making steel.  In virtue of his methodical habits and knowledge of accounts he was made secretary of this or that body or movement and for thirty years he was secretary of Brynhyfryd Chapel.  All this would, of course, be unpaid work.

He was in the fifties when I first remember him.  He occasionally took a pinch of snuff and at home smoked a churchwarden, lighting it at the kitchen fire from a supply of paper spills always available on the mantelpiece.  There would usually be a glass of beer within reach.  I was sent once a month, on Saturday afternoons to Penuel Row to have my hair cut by him.  I would be planted on a high stool in the centre of what was called " the bailey," a small paved enclosure opening out of the kitchen, and there the operation would take place.

He took an artist's pride in the result and I ran home refreshed. It was the age of hairpins, high combs and chignons for women and when small boys had their front hair curved into what my mother called a ' Q.P.' : which I take to have been a variant of toupee, perhaps through some mixing of a queue behind with a tuft in front. My mother used other words which puzzled me at the time. Tantrums was one ; trollop was another ; congees was a third, this last in the sense of showing off superior manners. She sent me to buy inkle not tape. Like Stephen Dedalus, she said tundish not funnel for the instrument through which oil is poured into a lamp. These words may have come with my grandmother from Somerset.

Enoch Jones carried himself so erect that it could be said of him as of another that in his port was the dignity of one who had borne His Majesty's Commission. It was ' the port of quality ' which eighteenth century epitaphs ascribe to the nobility. There was something aristocratic in his bearing which made him appear superior to his surroundings. It was not *hauteur* ; he was tender and compassionate. *Toujours chevaleresque* might have been his motto had he moved in knightly circles.

This distinction shone in the deacons pew in chapel where he guided the proceedings. The Welsh Presbyterian system was one in which a settled minister was the exception. Where the church had its own pastor he would preach at home on one Sunday in the month ; on the other Sundays he would be away and there would be " supplies " or visiting preachers in the pastor's place drawn from all over the Principality but normally from the surrounding counties. The renewal of invitations to visiting preachers was a matter of great delicacy, and was usually conducted in private either in chapel or in the chapelhouse after Sunday evening service. My grandfather (and after him my father) was the guardian of the *Diary* in which engagements were recorded for many years in advance. A good preacher would be pressed to promise two or more Sundays in the years to come ; a poor preacher would be fortunate if asked to return at all. My grandfather would gather informally the views of his fellow deacons and then himself decide what to do.

He had a discriminating taste in sermons ; his favourite preachers were Islwyn and Evan Phillips, both poets in different styles ; the one deriving from Milton and Wordsworth, the other a verbal goldsmith who dealt in sparkling jewels of thought, which he spread with great charm before his hearers. Words used by his biographer of Ruskin fit Evan Phillips perfectly : " The blue eyes piercing from beneath thick bushy eyebrows never ceased to shine with the fire of genius." But however mediocre the preacher my grandfather would find something to praise in the poorest sermon and his big heart would tend to a renewal of the invitation, not seldom to the vexation of his colleagues. His own speeches in church meetings invariably stressed the more genial aspects of the Gospel—God's love and mercy rather than man's frailty and sin. So did the hymns he chose. They were in the major key. He never groaned (as my father was apt to do) about the burden of the chapel debt. Standing erect he spoke out clearly so that all could hear every word he uttered ; he spoke buoyantly, kindling quickly and passing imperceptibly into a glowing eloquence and when we wished he would go on and on, he would stop suddenly and close the service with a triumphant hymn. It was the style of Evan Phillips. *Melle dulcior fluebat oratio.* Or a s the small rain upon the tender herb, and as the showers upon the grass. No one was bored and we all knew that when Enoch Jones presided at the week-night service it would last an hour precisely, however sinful the state of the world happened to be at that moment. Once when delegates came from the Monthly Meeting to look into the state of the " Cause " he was asked, *inter alia*, " Do the members attend divine service punctually ? " " We all leave punctually," he replied.

There were times when a deacon would pout and sulk and then his gifts as peacemaker would be in request. Persons in trouble naturally turned to him for help and comfort. He himself, with his sensitive and refined nature, had more than his fair share of private sorrow. He went bail for a friend who failed : the Bank foreclosed and he had to pay up. There was a clever and amusing son who died in the early thirties, his career mournfully wrecked by excessive drinking. There was an optimistic daughter who married an even more optimistic draper and the family savings had to be pooled and exhausted to prevent the disgrace of bankruptcy. Then one Sunday night in February, 1884, his brother, a ne'er-do-well tailor, was found dead in a ditch, badly bruised. He had been seen drunk on the previous evening. The contents of his pockets, his stockings, and a Sunday joint he was taking home, were found in the possession of a Patrick Callaghan. Callaghan was suspected of foul play and was tried at the Monmouth Assizes on a charge of wilful murder. Dr. Redwood declared that the wounds could not possibly have been caused by a series of falls. His Irish assistant declared that they could. Callaghan was acquitted. The verdict aroused great anger against the local Irish and riots were feared. Fifty policemen were drafted into the town and quartered in a local schoolroom. A Watch was stationed at the Armoury of the Volunteers. A detachment of the Welsh Regiment and a special train were held in readiness in Cardiff, but Callaghan and his parents fled out of the town, and the agitation died down.

My grandfather wore a brave countenance to the world but within grief kept gnawing at his heart strings and presently they snapped.  He was sixty-seven, and I chose for the black bordered mourning card this epitome of his character from one of the Pauline epistles : "But the end of the commandment is love out of a pure heart and a good conscience, and faith unfeigned.''

Much might be written of the other Brynhyfryd deacons. Daniel Hughes, the greengrocer, for example, was well read in the Puritan divines, knew the *Pilgrim's Progress* thoroughly and had soaked himself in Boston's *Fourfold State of Man* : innocence, depravity, recovery, happiness or misery.  This book is said to have had some influence on the style of Robert Louis Stevenson.  There was a Welsh translation.  Another favourite book of his was Gurnall's ingenious analysis and elaboration of the sixth chapter of the epistle to the Ephesians, *The Christian in Compleat Armour: a Treatise of the Saints' War against the Devil.*  A Welsh version of this had been printed at Trefecca in 1784.  One of this deacon's sons stayed away from chapel and became a Christadelphian which was almost as bad as becoming an atheist.  The village abounded in common and uncommon individuals whose portraits are stamped clearly on the memory after half a century.  Before my time there was Dewi Glan Taf, a stone cutter and poet, who wrote many epitaphs for the grave stones, and a popular interlude against the tyranny of the local parson who refused to admit grave-stones to the churchyard.  This dirge was publicly performed in the streets and the legend went that it caused the death of the

THE CHIEF DEACON:
ENOCH JONES, THE STORES

parson from a broken heart. And there was Gwilym Gelli Deg who left many poems scattered through various periodicals, the most popular of them being *Ble byddwn 'mhen can mlynedd?* (Where shall we be a hundred years hence?). Here are two stanzas for my Welsh readers :

Mae cael cyfeillach merched glân,
O fawr i fân yn fwyniant ;
A chael serchawgrwydd, llwydd, nid llai,
Na gorau'r rhai a'm carant ;
Pe cawn arglwyddes orau gwlad,
A'i thrysor rhad a'r orsedd,
A choron aur hoff ar ei phen,
B'le byddwn 'mhen can mlynedd ?

Beth fyddwn well pe cawn y dêr
Rif sêr o bob trysorau ;
Pe cawn y byd i gyd, mewn gair,
A dillad aur a pherlau ;
A chael y clodydd o bob gwlad,
Yn rhad a phob anrhydedd ;
Mewn palas aur a thŵr hyd nen,
B'le byddaf 'mhen can mlynedd ?

He left Rhymney for Merthyr and took to drink. And the sister of the local paper-hanger and glazier who had been bedridden for twenty-two years, but who, when suddenly her house took fire, leapt out of bed, and was completely cured.

Take a stretch of High Street. We lived in No. 100. Next door in No. 99, lived Evan Davies, cobbler and deacon, who learnt a chapter of the Bible weekly and recited it in Sunday School ; his son Ossian Gwent, patternmaker, poet, and deacon. With them lodged the Rev. Edward Davies, an educational pioneer and an active controversialist, who addressed a pamphlet to Mr. Gladstone in which he pleaded for Intermediate Education for Wales, and wrote another denouncing Bible teaching in Board Schools, called *Caesar or God.* Through 136 pages, beginning with Cain and Abel, one verse after another is adduced to prove that "all degrees of legal coercion—in connection with any degree of religion—belong to the stings of the locusts mentioned in the Revelation, and to the mystic Babylon ' drunken with the blood of the martyrs of Jesus '." At No. 98 lived Mrs. Evans, " Llwyni ", a buxom widow with pink complexion, attired in black silk, engaged in selling Welsh flannel. No. 97 was a boot and shoe shop, managed by Twynog Jeffreys, cobbler, poet, journalist, raconteur. For years he wrote a column to a weekly journal published at Aberdare, *Tarian y Gweithiwr* (The Workman's Shield). In his later years he was wheeled about, crippled by rheumatism, but his genial humour and love of gossip never forsook him. Next door at No. 96, lived the Rev. T. E. Edwards, a steel worker turned preacher, with a gruff voice. His sermons were marked with a boldness of imaginative treatment which made him popular with the fervent Welsh congregations. His son, with whom I played, rose to be the President of the Co-operative Congress. At No. 95 lived a musical family, one of whom we have met before as the *Nightingale of Monmouthshire (Eos Mynwy).* His brother was the precentor at Brynhyfryd, who closed his eyes the better to hear the tuning fork, and opened them when the tune was safely launched. His predecessor as precentor had been Heman Gwent (1823-1878), bookseller and postmaster, and one of the first in Wales to conduct the *Messiah* with a full orchestra. Then finally at No. 94, where the street was interrupted, Tobias Fine conducted a pawnbroking business and he could have truthfully displayed a card in his window : Welsh Spoken. All these neighbours of ours were distinct personalities, not a row of postage stamps. They were active not passive citizens.

Nothing in the village was alien to them. They were interested and themselves interesting. They were the teachers in that "university of real life" into which my grandfather plunged me at fourteen.

### (iii) PREACHERS

*Salvation was his song,*
*Free grace his only theme ;*
*He fled this howling vale,*
*His eyes behold the gleam.*

Epitaph on tomb of REV. EDWIN JONES.

BETWEEN the years of sixteen and twenty I was a voracious reader. Unlike those of the Time Office, conditions in the Mill Office and the Cashiers' Office were not favourable to surreptitious reading in working hours. My leisure was further curtailed by chapel services. But at home I enjoyed a special dispensation and was allowed to read at meals. And it was not necessary to go to bed before one o'clock.

I have in an earlier chapter described the founding of our public library in the fifties which in 1905 was to expand into the Workmen's Institute. The original house was dull and dingy, and the contents of the shelves were cased in uniform black buckram, which destroyed any variety of colour in the original. Two books from the shelves which fascinated me at some stage were a *Life of Napoleon* by E. Gifford and the *History of the Jews* by Josephus. But I relied mainly on the weekly volume of Cassell's *National Library* which introduced me to Shakespeare and all the chief poets; to Plutarch's *Lives*, to the *Diary* of Pepys, to the *Sermons* of Latimer, to Johnson's *Lives of the Poets*, to Silvio Pellico and the story of his imprisonment; to the *Sorrows of Werther*,

to the *Angel in the House* and to most of what was worth while in
the whole realm of English literature and such classics as had
undergone translation.    As my wages increased I advanced from
the paper edition at threepence to the sixpenny edition in cloth.
I discovered the fascination of second-hand catalogues and
became then and have continued ever since a modest customer
of Thomas Thorp of Guildford and Old Bond Street.    There
were also, I found out somehow, bargains to be had from booksellers in Edinburgh, especially in the field of theology, where I
was increasingly finding congenial pabulum.    This appetite was
fostered by the Sunday School examinations with their prescribed
commentaries in Welsh published annually by the Calvinistic
Methodist Bookroom at Caernarvon.    For a population of
less than a million speaking the language, the Welsh had an
inordinate supply of commentaries, their numbers largely swollen
by sectarian divisions.    In 1867 there were nine commentaries on
the whole Bible, exclusive of several family Bibles, with practical
and devotional notes for family reading ; nine on the New Testament separately ; several on particular books of the Bible, with a
large number of works on oriental customs, Biblical antiquities,
natural history, and geography.    There were, besides, eight Biblical
and theological dictionaries, seven or eight systems of theology,
and works without number on practical and devotional subjects.
One Congregational minister had accomplished the Herculean
task of translating, printing, and publishing the voluminous
commentary of Matthew Henry on the Bible.    I began with the
easy commentaries of Albert Barnes, then widely used throughout Wales, but I quickly advanced to the works of Westcott and
Lightfoot and valiantly tackled the ponderous tomes of German
theologians published in Edinburgh by T. & T. Clark.    I recall
struggling  valiantly  with  the  works  of  Dorner  and  Martensen

in particular. Fortunately there were available the more easily digested handbooks written by the scholarly ministers of the Free Church of Scotland, the most absorbing in my recollection being a study of the Reformation by Dr. T. M. Lindsay, the father of the present Master of Balliol.

My most presumptuous enterprise was an analysis of the *Systematic Theology* of Dr. Charles Hodge of Princeton, one of the leading Calvinistic divines of that period. It was a magisterial work in three volumes and it surveyed the history of man " from everlasting to everlasting ". Hodge rejected the definition of theology as the science of religion and restricted it to the science concerned with the facts and principles of the Bible. This initial limitation determined the range of his exposition. I could not possibly have understood, except superficially, much of what I read in my teens but I certainly found satisfaction in it. The doctrine may have been arid but it was not sloppy like some of the evangelicalism which followed it. One went daily to the office, did one's work properly and without exhaustion and all the time the mind dwelt in an inner world of thought and speculation. Doubt and criticism came later but earlier it was comforting to find a plan of salvation, an intelligible interpretation of human history which seemed logical and conclusive. This plan was conceived in terms of jurisprudence, this being the science in the ascendant when the fathers of the Latin Church began to formulate their theology. And Calvin had been trained in the civil law. God was sovereign, omnipotent, infinite, and judge of all the world. Man was finite, fallen, a guilty sinner. The law had been broken ; atonement must be made ; Christ offered himself and satisfied the demands of divine justice. Hodge's major difference from Calvin lay in his assertion of man's free will, which Calvin denied.

My enthusiasm for the study of theology did not escape the notice of the deacons at Brynhyfryd and they encouraged me to prepare for the ministry of the Church. I was nothing loth. No Civil Service examination for which I could sit was in sight. I had never known any specific memorable experience that could be dignified with the name of conversion. I had moved forward into church membership in the regular manner of young persons brought up in a religious home. I was already helping my grandfather with the accounts, acting as secretary to various projects for reducing the chapel debt, active in the local debating society and never absent from a chapel service. The pulpit was my manifest destiny, and in 1890 I was accepted by the monthly meeting as a candidate for the ministry. Motives are always mixed and I was neither better nor worse than scores of my contemporaries in Wales who found in preaching at once the escape from routine and a field for the exercise of unused powers in unselfish service.

We have it on the authority of the *Encyclopaedia Britannica* that the appetite of the Welsh people for sermons is enormous. It would not be a gross exaggeration to apply to the Wales of my youth a sentence from the *Dialogue on Oratory* by Tacitus :

"With them moreover it was a conviction that without eloquence it was impossible for anyone either to attain to a position of distinction and prominence in the community or to maintain it."

Nor was this a new or passing characteristic. It is on record from as far back as the days of Cato that the Celts delighted in oratory and from the days of Giraldus that they delighted in music.

In the years preceding the Evangelical Revival of the 18th century it is said that preachers dealt with men as reasonable

persons but during and after the Revival as sinners. With
the latter type of ministry went a disparagement of learning. An
illiterate pulpit and an illiterate congregation went together.
There were always among the early Welsh preachers a few
men of great natural ability whose thought and imagery were
of an exalted order, but there was also much extragavance and
superstition, much sound and fury signifying little or nothing
in the preaching of the revivalists. What John Selden wrote
of England was no less true of Wales : " Preaching by the
Spirit (as they call it) is most esteemed by the common people
because they cannot abide art or learning, which they have not
been bred up in—so they say to the preachers ' you come with
your school learning : there's such a one has the Spirit.' " But
as I have stated in an earlier chapter, scholars like Thomas
Charles of Bala and later Lewis Edwards were deeply convinced
of the necessity of an educated ministry. Bala College was
founded in 1839 and Trevecca in 1842. These two seminaries
had year after year sent forth a proportion of able, educated,
and dedicated men to serve the Calvinistic Methodist churches.
And of all the best preachers in the seventies and eighties it
could be said that the secret of their influence lay in the perfect
fusion of intellect and passion.

The peripatetic system brought a great variety of gospellers
to the pulpit of Brynhyfryd in the course of a year. It was a
poor church and could not therefore command the more gifted
preachers except at the special services called " Great Meetings."
We heard the rank and file of the ministers settled in the county
of Monmouth and just over the border in Glamorgan. Some
of these had minds of a limited range and made up for the lack
of matter in ways which amused their youthful listeners. One
made great play with his spectacles placing them carefully on

the nose, removing them slowly and resting them reverently on the open Bible, replacing them on the nose and repeating the sequence throughout the expository introduction to the sermon. Another would not take his overcoat off in the pulpit until the congregation was singing the hymn immediately before the sermon. We guessed the number of times A.B. would appeal to ' my brethren ', the number of times B. C. would raise his hand slowly from the Bible to touch his right ear, the number of minutes C. D. would take to reach the end after announcing ' a few words in conclusion '. D. E. had a whining voice and E. F. a frequent grunt or cough, emitting each phrase with difficulty through a narrow passage. There were preachers with amplitude of body, penury of mind, and copiousness of sound, who shouted Mesopotamia, Tierra del Fuego and Pocahontas. " And he was gifted most that loudest baul'd." There were those who spoke hardly above a whisper and you strained to hear them for they had a message ; there were those who read essays ; there were those who had a dental delivery, all emphasis, clipping each word with their teeth. There were those who offered the gospel in a jaunty fashion like auctioneers and who handled the greatest mysteries of the faith without misgiving and whose cocksureness was offensive. There were preachers who filled the pulpit with shavings and produced a blazing flame for a minute ; it died down suddenly and left no trace behind. There were massive theologians who delivered weighty and memorable sermons, illuminating some dark doctrinal problem, taking fifty minutes to do so. There were those who discovered a spiritual symbolism in the nails of the tabernacle. There were ' sweet ' preachers, trembling on the verge of metre, of whom it was said that they sold Everton toffee. There were those who were grave and gay in the course of the same sermon and had their audience alternately dissolved in laughter and tears. Some carried drollery in the pulpit to indecorous lengths and turned the service into mere entertainment. There were those who conformed to the orthodox description : who began low, went on slow, rose higher and struck fire, resorting to all the varieties of rhythm, rising, falling, waved and level, and thereby evoking all the emotional power which resides in a liturgical language like the Welsh. Others poured out a torrential flood of ideas from the reading of the text onwards to the close—Dr. Owen Prys for example, when fresh from Cambridge. Some were masters of metaphor and illustration. I never remember hearing a political sermon in Brynhyfryd, though that was a charge commonly made by Anglicans against nonconformists. And I am writing of a time when the Welsh pulpit did not directly relate the Incarnation to problems of housing and drainage, wages and strikes, sweating and tariffs. As I suggested above the preachers most revered were men of great parts, whose fame was restricted by the language they used, in whom learning, devotion, reverence, passion, imagination, an instinctive feeling for the right word, the rhythmic sentence and the melodious delivery, were blended with such subtle yet spontaneous and compelling art that to listen to their oratory induced emotions comparable to those we experience when we hear the *Fifth Symphony* or the *Mass in B Minor*.

But sometimes even ordinary services would turn out to be extraordinary. On some unforeseen Sunday evening at Brynhyfryd when there would be present only the usual small congregation of the regular and faithful members, and when the preacher would be nobody in particular, some verse of a hymn, some petition in a prayer, some phrase in the sermon, would suddenly bring preacher and hearers together into a harmony of mood ; the little preacher would rise above himself, words would drop from his lips like the dew of Hermon, the heavens opened and poor old folk saw a light shining on their hard road and felt their lives had an immortal quality and were part of the divine order of the world.    They returned to their humble homes comforted.    " Human beings are never so happy, so soothed, so unafraid as when they seem to identify themselves with the Ruling Mind."    If it was dope, it was at least the dope of love and not of hate.

# CHAPTER XI

## BEAUTY

*Rhymney is perhaps the least attractive spot in a district not too remarkable for sweetness and light. It is merely a congested collection of mean cottages at the bottom of a barren valley and has little to show in the way of modern conveniences.*

METHUEN's *Little Guides*, 1909, p. 222.

THERE are few countries in the world more naturally beautiful than Wales and few in which industry and morality have been more indifferent to the claims of beauty. I was not actually conscious of this fact in my youth. I did not, as Traherne would have us do, wake every morning in heaven and feel myself in my Father's palace. I did not feel the attraction of the hills which enclosed the village; though these, near at hand, were heaps of blue slag dumped from the furnaces in years gone by, smoothed and rounded by time and thinly fringed with anaemic blades of yellow-pale grass. Further afield I could find whinberries and lie on my back on the green turf listening to the larks, or sit on the banks of a mountain stream weaving bulrushes into whips or into love knots, or whittling away an ash twig while watching the landscape winking and shimmering through the heat. These were Saturday afternoons and they filled the heart with happiness. Like the rest of mankind we experienced in Rhymney the alternations of night and day and witnessed, or might have witnessed, the miracle of the dawn and the slow procession of the stars. I do not remember doing this, and in a village where the works of man did little to supply the need for beauty it is odd I did not turn more hungrily to nature.

> ' The stars still write their golden purposes
> On heaven's high palimpsest and no man sees '

There were nowhere buildings to stir an aesthetic emotion except the tall chimney stacks which evoked a boy's admiration by their proportions, their dizzy height, and the skill with which brick had been laid on brick, and the overpowering number of bricks. Tips, tunnels, tramroads, dumps of old brick and stone, and an indescribable litter of scrap iron abutted on the dwelling houses. The churchyard was in the main street and every grave so full that no room could be found for another corpse. Locomotives went to and fro, puffing and panting, all through the day and night, moving trucks of coal and iron ore and steel rails and tin bars from this place to that, banging the buffers and couplings together in a discordant symphony. This engine was hissing and spitting, that one blowing steam off; the great mechanical hammers pounded away like some elemental natural force. There was no end to the clatter and clangour. There was never any silence; there is now. One sight always thrilled us. In the blackest night the cupola-furnace at " the Bessemer " would suddenly open its great maw, light the heavens, throw up molten jewels which fell in a cascade of golden rain. Then just as suddenly darkness closed over us blacker than ever.

When I recall what then seemed to me beautiful I think of Mr. Dixon's chemist shop with its pleasant scent and globes of coloured glass and rows of strange names, in gilt letters, the words broken up into bits. Mr. and Mrs. Dixon—we spoke of them with respect—were English and childless. They had learnt Welsh but kept themselves to themselves and were always as neat and spotless in their dress and person as the jars on their shelves. I visited their shop periodically with a penny and came away with sweets like golden sovereigns or with tamarind fruit which I called tambourine.

I remember feeling an emotional response to the cottage gardens in sowing time. The thriftier colliers took a pride in these, plotting them out with the aid of string and sticking the coloured seed packets in the pegs. When presently the plants sprouted in regular lines their symmetrical perfection stirred pleasant sensations in the passers-by.

> And Jones was planting seedlings all about,
> Supremely
> Geometrically right
> For all to see . . . .
> All in a rhythm reachless by modernity.

In the cottage windows there would be pots of geraniums and fuchsias, droppers as we called them, and in the garden beds of pansies, sweet-williams, mignonette, stocks, old man, nasturtiums, and lilies of the valley.

Rechabite prejudice did not destroy though it diminished one's enjoyment of the well-groomed dray horses emerging in twos and threes from the yard of the brewery in shining harness straining their giant limbs as they went up the hill towards High Street laden with barrels of beer.

Such were the simple visual delights of our childhood on which our eyes loved to linger. Of painting, sculpture, architecture, there was little to behold beyond the portraits of Spurgeon, the one-eyed Christmas Evans and Garibaldi in his red shirt. The familiar faces in the street were not distinguished for physical beauty. Those of the miners were often scarred and marred with blue bruises and the absence of an eye, an arm, or a leg was not uncommon. The women bore the marks of poverty and hard labour. I thought the brickyard girls and the pit-head girls bonnier than the domesticated variety. Perhaps they were only saucier. Whatever their blemishes courtship flourished in lanes and passages and at back doors and presently couples were discovered 'keeping company' and 'walking out' and this perambulation might go on and on for as long as a windjammer's voyage. There were occasional disasters when the unbridled unfortunates were caught and branded as with scarlet letters. It was not at once that I understood that an affiliation case, for so it was always spoken of in the local press, was a journalist's cloak for bastardy. Excitement of another kind was provided by cheap railway and boat excursions to Weston-Super-Mare and Ilfracombe. I was not myself a witness of the Welsh deacon returning with a Sunday School excursion on the paddleboat from Ilfracombe in a storm who in his sick agonies was heard petitioning the Almighty to be allowed to die on shore as he had a plot bought and *paid for* in the churchyard at home. For six shillings you could travel to and from the Belle Vue Gardens, Manchester, if you were prepared to leave Rhymney at an unearthly hour on Saturday morning and return at a more heavenly hour on Sunday. London was then a long way off. The Severn Tunnel dates from 1886. A journey to London was a local event quickly noised abroad. My father returned from his first visit with his hair and beard so stylishly trimmed that his children had some difficulty in recognising him.

The domestic and working lives of every family were inter-locked within an iron framework and ordered by the

Company's hooter which blew daily, without hesitation or variability, precisely at five-thirty and at six in the morning; at eight-fifteen and at nine; at one and at two; and finally at six o'clock in the evening. Passenger trains on their way to and from Cardiff, twenty-four miles away, pulled up daily at the railway station at the same times year in and year out and the engines snorted and sneezed at the same precise intervals while waiting for the guard's signal.

Professor Whitehead has since told us that unless civilization is permeated through and through with routine, civilization vanishes. Rhymney was a pillar of civilization by day and a cloud of civilization by night. The stuff of human life poured into moulds of conduct and habit from childhood like the molten metal from the smelting furnace into ingots and pigs. We did not philosophize on the nature of work; we did not ask whether it was an evil or a religious duty, a curse or expiation. We did not then demand the right to work though we did try to reduce the hours of labour. Work was our settled destiny. The two or three who could afford to ' retire ' did so (a publican, a shopkeeper, an insurance agent) and this showed what most of us would like to do. But we had to content ourselves with lying in bed on Sunday mornings, that blessed and holy and hooterless day of rest.

Sport bulked far less in our lives then than since and Leisure was a plank in no party programme. Nor did we dare to hope for an economic millenium on the earth. Our Utopia was elsewhere. For us the judgment of this world was not a remote contingency but an impending doom. In my first Welsh reading book I was forbidden to love the world or ought that is within it. " Hold the fort for I am coming " was the most popular children's hymn.

Nothing changed but the weather and it changed for the worse. Rain was the rule. We were nearly a thousand feet up from the sea. To the north of us the hills rose a further thousand feet into the Brecon Beacons. It did not merely shower, it poured, or in the local tongue it rained cats and dogs. Sudden squalls swept wildly through the streets tumbling the ash buckets noisily pell-mell along the pavements. Shop windows took on a dismal dreariness and the goods seen through the misty panes looked shoddier and shabbier than ever. Row upon row of houses was soaked in a deceptive melancholy, deceptive because behind the closed doors hospitable fires were burning. Coal was cheap and plentiful and made for cheerfulness in the poorest home on the gloomiest day. And likely enough if it was evening the father would be entertaining the family with a saga of his adventures in the mine or his encounters with the whimsicalities of the machine he was tending. I have listened time and again to the affectionate talk of a mechanic describing the behaviour of an old pit pump, her moods and tenses, her crotchets and tantrums, as if he were telling of a sweetheart or a mistress. Such hazardous adventure and vivid companionship in mill and pit went some way to slake the thirst for beauty and excitement in the ordinary man.

Fortunately for many there were the joys of choral music, which I have already described, and for the few there was the traditional delight in poetry which enabled working men to dabble in the intricacies of Welsh versification; lampooning or complimenting each other, or celebrating the birth or marriage, death or recovery of a neighbour, in four-line stanzas of an intricate pattern of alliteration and assonance. Here is an example by Thomas Probert, a Brynhyfryd deacon, in praise of the bellows, with an English version made for me by Dr. Idris Bell :

Y fegin gulfin gelfydd—-yr aelwyd
A siriola beunydd
Y tân, i'w ben, t'wynu bydd
O dyniad ei hadenydd.

The thin-lipped tool which to a cheerful glow
The whole hearth brings
As the fire leaps to gusty flame below
Its pulsing wings.

For the rest, for the rank and file, the poor and lowly, the simple and the humble, there was always the moral beauty of truth and goodness, perceived by the eye of faith, the consolations of religion, the Kingdom of God, of which they learnt from sermon and hymn and the Bible itself. The fleeting nature of this present world, its infection with sin, a fact which they could verify by looking into their own hearts, the redeeming mission of Christ, the transfiguring work of the Holy Spirit as evidenced by holy living here, the assurance of immortal life hereafter in a spiritual world—all this was taught, as I have said earlier, through every variety of metaphor and illustration and by every gift of oratory and song.

" A'r gwleddoedd maith sydd yn parhau
Lle nid oes gofid, poen na gwae."

Heaven was real and it was beautiful and if we thought of it in material images that was natural. It was a King's palace and it had grand parlours with comfortable couches and cushions and great halls for Welsh choirs. And chiefly it was a haven of rest after toil, port after stormy seas. It did not occur to us, as it did to an Aberdeen preacher, to think of it as a place of " abundant and remunerative employment." We knew little enough of remuneration, but of employment we had had more than enough.

N

Railway

Road to
Tredegar and
Abergavenny.

Llechryd

Graig Cemetery

Chapel

To Blaen · Rhymney

Rhymney Bridge
Station

Rhymney
House

× Old Furnace

Rhymney
River

Newtown

Reservoir

Road to
Merthyr

Lucas Shop
and
House

Ebenezer
Chapel

High Street

Penuel
Chapel

Upper School

Brick
Tile W

Zion
Chapel

Cemetery

Railway

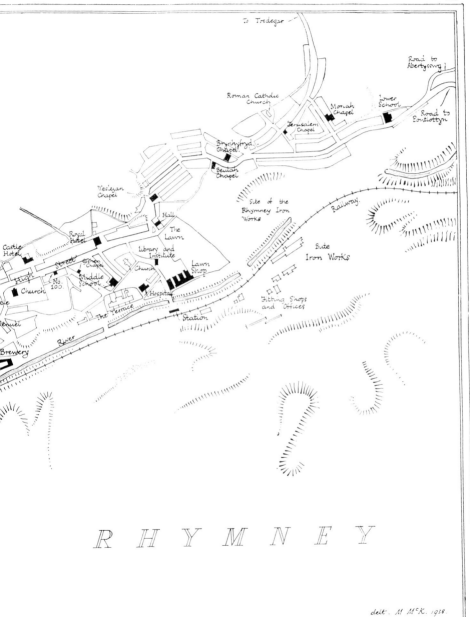

To Tredegar

Road to Abertysswg

Roman Catholic Church

Lower School

Road to Pontlottyn

Moriah Chapel

Jerusalem Chapel

Brynhyfryd Chapel

Beulah Chapel

Wesleyan Chapel

Site of the Rhymney Iron Works

Railway

Hall

The Lawn

Castle Hotel

Royal Hotel

Bute Iron Works

Library and Institute

High Street

Ebenezer Chapel

Church

Lawn Shop

Church

No. 100.

Middle School

Hospital

Fitting Shops and Offices

The Terrace

Station

Kennel

River

Brewery

R H Y M N E Y

delt. M MᶜK. 1938.